The Future of Leisure Services:
Thriving on Change

For Cassandra

The Future of
Leisure Services:
Thriving on Change

Geoffrey C. Godbey

Venture Publishing, Inc.
State College, Pennsylvania

Production Supervision by Bonnie Godbey
Cover Design by Sandra Sikorski
Editorial Assistance, Desktop Publishing by Deborah Kerstetter
Library of Congress Catalogue Card Number: 88-51574
ISBN: 0-910251-30-4

About the Author

Geoffrey Godbey is Professor of Recreation and Parks at The Pennsylvania State University. He is the author of five books concerning leisure and leisure services: *Leisure Studies and Services: An Overview,* with Stanley Parker; *Recreation, Park and Leisure Services: Foundations, Organization, Administration; Leisure in Your Life: An Exploration; The Evolution of Leisure: Historical and Philosophical Perspectives,* with Thomas Goodale; and *The Future of Leisure Services: Thriving on Change.* Godbey has written for a wide variety of academic, practitioner, and mass market publications including *The Journal of Leisure Research, The Nation, Public Opinion, World Tennis, Parks and Recreation,* and others. He has served as an associate editor and reviewer for a number of journals and is the Managing Editor of Venture Publishing, Inc., a publishing house concerned with leisure-related literature. Research and writing undertaken by Dr. Godbey have been presented on the *Today Show, ABC Evening News, U.S. News and World Report, Science Digest, Chronicle of Higher Education, Wall Street Journal, New York Times,* and elsewhere.

Godbey has conducted research pertaining to leisure behavior and older people-- most recently, a nationwide study of the use of local parks by older people in urban areas. Other research interests include public recreation planning and evaluation, leisure behavior patterns, time budgets, commercial recreation and leisure services, and philosophies of leisure.

Formerly, Godbey was Acting Chairman, Department of Recreation, at the University of Waterloo; Instructor-in-Charge of the Recreation Leadership Curriculum for inner-city students at the Ogontz Campus at Penn State, near Philadelphia; and a Research Intern with the Philadelphia Department of Recreation. He has also been Visiting Research Professor at the University of Salford in Salford, England. Godbey was a consultant to the U.S. Department of Interior for three years in the development of the Third Nationwide Outdoor Recreation Plan. He was President of the

Academy of Leisure Sciences in 1987-88 and President of the Society of Park and Recreation Educators in 1988-89. A member of the Board of Directors of the World Leisure and Recreation Association, he has given invited presentations in 16 countries.

He is the author of a book of poetry and has published widely in literary magazines. An avid tennis and squash player, Godbey has consulted for a wide variety of public and commercial agencies concerned with recreation, parks, and leisure services.

Preface

Today, technology is accelerating change in all stations of our lives. Some life prolonging and others life threatening—such as the destruction of our environment. The complexity of the demographic changes occuring in our society makes one question what the composition of our society will be in the near future. These rapid changes dictate an urgent assessment for future leisure needs.

The author has undertaken this difficult task in a clear and concise manner. He has bridged the gap of identifying changes in our society and their impact upon leisure service delivery systems. He challenges all segments of the leisure profession: educators, researchers, programmers and managers alike to deal with the future today.

This book is required reading by all individuals who are involved in leisure services.

R. Dean Tice
Executive Director
National Recreation and
Park Association

Contents

INTRODUCTION

It is hard to imagine how fast the rate of change in our society is accelerating. If we represent all the time that has elapsed since the beginning of our universe as a single year, then the extensive use of science and technology by human beings began only during the last second of the last minute of the last day of that year (Sagan, 1977). This literal explosion in knowledge has produced unprecedented change in the way we live, the ways in which we affect the rest of the universe, and how we define ourselves. It has also changed and will continue to change our concepts of recreation and leisure and what we want from these spheres of life.

Those of us in recreation, park and leisure services are in the process of fundamentally altering what we do, how we do it and why. Change is the one "constant" of our emerging profession. We will either change of our own accord, be forced to change or disappear. Some traditional leisure services are disappearing, but so gradually that those involved often don't know it is happening. It is time to rethink, experiment and go in some new directions. There is no use dragging your feet; the car is going 500 miles an hour.

This brief book is an attempt to document some of the ways in which our society is changing and to examine some of the ways that these changes will shape leisure services in the future (the future starting tomorrow). I have written this book because, during the last year, I have had the pleasure of speaking to recreation, park and leisure service professionals in a variety of settings concerning present and future trends and their impact upon our field. At these presentations, a number of people came up afterwards and said: "You should write a book about this." I have.

SECTION ONE — CHANGES

Not only is our world characterized by extremely rapid change, but each change identified, like a complex design of rows of dominoes, quickly ripples through the rest of society and the environment. Our desire for cheap hamburger, for instance, affects the amount of rain forest in Central America (cut down to make grazing land) which affects the earth's atmosphere in a number of ways which affect the incidence of skin cancer which affect the outdoor leisure patterns of older Americans which affect the demand for leisure services which affects the management patterns of public recreation and park professionals. Every human act has become a stone thrown into the water, causing ripples throughout the universe.

In effect, this means that every change is relevant in terms of shaping the future. Such a situation makes it almost impossible to write a brief book about such changes, since the author needs to know about everything. Additionally, where does one begin and end? The following changes are presented, not on the assumption that they are the only important ones, but that they are, at least, significant. It is left to the reader to judge their ultimate comparative impact.

Some will find the changes identified as presenting a somewhat pessimistic picture of our times. Among recreation, park and leisure service professionals, this is sometimes equated with lack of faith. Our profession is, by nature, positive. While I confess a bias toward the positive, the reading and thinking I have done about the future in the last few years lead me to the conclusion that we are going to have to stare some very unpleasant realities in the face during the next decade. We are living above our means, we are fouling our own nest, we have forgotten our own children, we are ignorant of the rest of the world, we think it is admirable to be rich in the face of homelessness.

The following section contains too many statistics and not enough order. You must cipher through it and come to your own conclusions. In the second section, I have come to a few conclusions of my own concerning how these changes will shape our field and how we will help shape the future.

Generations in Conflict

Today our society contains three generations of adults with very differing life experiences and views of the world. The oldest generation, born before 1920, survived the Great Depression. Most have been through two world wars. Many of them moved from farms and other rural residences to urban areas as the nation industrialized. This generation was very often the sons and daughters of immigrants. They married late and had small families. Economic considerations were often the overriding consideration in whether or not a marriage could take place. In this aspect they were like their European predecessors, who also married late. For example, Pollock (1987) reported that between 1600 and 1900 in Britain, "Demographers have conclusively shown that the average age of first marriage was commonly in the late twenties for men, and the mid-twenties for women" (Pollock, 1987). A second generation, born between 1920 and 1940, entered adulthood during a period of unparalleled affluence and optimism about the future. They married early, bought large cars and houses, pushed for civil rights, and had large families. Many moved from cities to the rapidly developing suburbs. Today, many of this generation are divorced. A younger generation, born during the "boom" years that began during World War II, began to settle in central cities and small towns, the areas deserted by their parents. Their economic outlooks were somewhat less bright than their parents. More women of this generation have put independence and work before marriage and child-rearing. Many have married late or not at all.

While for the first generation recreation was often considered sinful or was limited to activities which cost little, the middle generation often thought their leisure was "earned" by work. They began to spend money on leisure and to have "fun." For the younger generation, leisure is less tied to work and, often, more a source of individual meaning or self-definition. It is also thought of as a "right" which need not always be earned. These three generations, with their widely contrasting life experiences and orientations, form a society which cannot speak with one voice on most issues because of the conflicting evidence with which their lives have provided them. The next generation of adults to join these three will also differ from the others. This new generation will be poorer economically, more conservative and, perhaps, less well educated.

Changing Styles of Life
Since World War II

After the horrors of the Great Depression and two world wars,
America entered a period of unprecedented economic prosperity.
Primarily because of the devastation of our manufacturing competitors in the world, such as England, France, Germany and
others, and due to the huge manufacturing capability we had
developed to support our war effort, the United States became the
world's strongest economy. In Canada, lucrative opportunities for
foreign investment meant that Canadians would temporarily lose
control of their own economy. The value orientation which fueled
our economic growth was the Protestant Ethic. "Self-denial, self-
sacrifice, conformity, and devotion to home, family and job were
the order of the day" (Yankelovich, Skelly and White, 1986).
Leisure activities were largely home-based and viewed as opportunities to be productive as well as have fun. The middle-class
expanded to include 70 percent of the population. Home ownership became more prevalent with such affluence.

By the 1960s, people had adjusted to this increased affluence and developed a "psychology of affluence" (Yankelovich,
Skelly and White, 1986). Under this belief system, people began
to assume that affluence would continue to increase indefinitely.
The old notion of sacrifice and self-denial gave way to interest in
self-fulfillment, with emphasis upon a broad range of involvement
in leisure experiences, often outside the family unit. Child-rearing
became more permissive. Financial and moral constraints were
less and less important.

New economic constraints developed in the 1970s, including recessions, inflation and unemployment. During this period,
the thrust toward a broad range of leisure experiences as a means
of personal fulfillment began to weaken. We also began to recognize some of the problems associated in shifting from a "we" to a
"me" mentality, such as the consequences of divorce and a weakening sense of community. This era brought about a reassessment

of values and expectations. "Adjusting to a 'new Realism,' consumers began to recognize that they could not do it all, have it all, be it all; instead, doing what is 'possible' and 'important' became the predominant approach" (Yankelovich, Skelly and White, 1986). The home became more important again both for escape from the problems of society and as a source of leisure activity. Many individuals, having narrowed their range of participation in leisure activities, began to specialize in a few activities with more emphasis upon acquiring skills and knowledge.

During the 1980s, people have begun to lower their expectations somewhat concerning both the economy and what it is possible for government to accomplish. Self-reliance has become a more central value. There has not been a return to the Protestant Ethic but rather a pragmatic attempt to blend the new values of the 1960s and 1970s with new economic realities. There is a great attempt to maximize resources of time and money. The line between work and leisure is becoming more permeable. In leisure, as in the rest of life, Yankelovich, Skelly and White noted an emphasis upon skill and performance, mastery and winning. The leisure consumer has become more critical and selective. It is the era of the "bottom line" in many areas of life. It is an era, too, in which we are recognizing that we are one country among many, a country with massive debts, drug problems, and an educational system in need of an overhaul. While there is some emphasis upon simplifying lives, many people are running faster and faster just to stay in place economically. A number of social and environmental problems have been put, temporarily, on hold. In their heart of hearts, many people understand we are going to go through a process of fundamental change.

A Rapidly Aging Society

Our society is getting older and older at a rapid rate. In this respect, we are like most other nations who have undergone extensive industrialization: birthrates decline and those who are born live longer. This does not mean that our population will stay where it is; it is already predicted that the United States will reach 350 million in a few decades. It does mean that every aspect of our society is being rapidly changed by the life situations of older citizens. For the first time, the average (median) age of a United States resident is over 32 years old (U.S. Census Bureau, 1987). The fastest growing age group in our society is the 35- to 44 year-olds, the leading edge of the Baby Boom Generation. The next fastest growing groups are those 85 and over, and those 75 to 84 years old. The percentage of people age 65 and over is also likely to increase from 12.1 percent of the population to 21.2 percent during the next 42 years (AARP, 1987). There will be almost 35 million persons age 65 or older in the year 2000 (see Figure 1). About one-half of all women age 65 and over are widowed, over three times the percentage of elderly men. Nine out of ten elderly people are white.

Those who reach old age at the beginning of the twenty-first century are likely to be increasingly diverse in their medical, economic, psychological and social characteristics. Those who are poor in their old age will make increasing demands on their families and such families will be smaller, thus increasing the burden on an individual basis. Those who are prosperous or have good pensions may move closer to the ideal of living a life of leisure than at any time in the past.

This rapid aging has produced many problems and many benefits for our society. Because we have been "youth-oriented," we have been slow to respond to an aging population. Many of us carry stereotypes in our head which no longer apply. The 55 to 64 age group in our society today has more financial assets than any other. The age of 65 means less and less in terms of retirement since only about one out of four workers continues working until forced, by law, to retire. The life situations of the elderly are becoming more and more diverse and labeling individuals by age makes increasingly less sense, although we continue to do so.

Figure 1
Number of Persons 65 or Older: 1900 to 2030

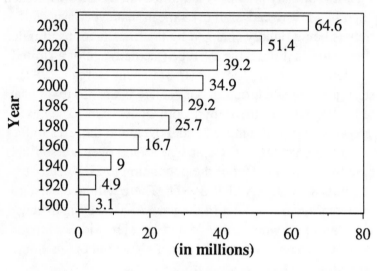

Note: Increments in years on vertical scale are uneven
Based on data from U.S. Bureau of the Census

Federal spending on the elderly now accounts for approximately one-half of the $623 billion domestic budget, up from one-third two decades ago. In 1986, about 13 percent of those 65 years and older lived below the poverty line while 20 percent of children under 18 years of age lived in poverty (U.S. Census Bureau, 1988). Because those over the age of 65 are far more likely to vote than any other age group, they are becoming a political power to be reckoned with. (For example, 31 percent of 25- to 29-year-olds vote while 65 percent of those 65 and over vote.) In spite of this new-found political power, many elderly live just above the poverty line and face problems of crime, housing, health care and prejudice in a society which often has little respect for age.

One great benefit of our aging society may be in the area of crime. Since roughly one-half of all the crime committed in the country is committed by males under the age of 25, as we age, crime rates may drop. Such increased public safety would have great implication for many forms of leisure activity, which are often undertaken by older people only if they feel safe in doing so.

Because our society is composed of generations which have had distinctly different life experiences, the next generation of elderly will be quite different from those who are now old. Progressive generations of elderly will have increasingly higher levels of education, better health, a broader variety of leisure interests and decidedly higher levels of expectations concerning what life should hold. Our children will have to break away from the mentality produced by the industrialization process which assumed that after formal education a person either worked or became a homemaker until the age of 65, at which time the worker retired since he or she was no longer economically useful. This way of thinking has been obsolete for a long time (perhaps as long as it has existed). People change dramatically over the life course. In many ways, as we grow older we become more different from each other rather than more alike. "Senior citizen" is a term which has obscured our need to plan more inclusively for later life. It has segregated those 65 and over from the rest of society. This segregation makes less and less sense in a society where the age of 65 tells us less and less about an individual's working status, economic status, health status or leisure interests.

As the Baby Boom Generation ages, it is likely to fundamentally change our methods of health care delivery. Since this highly educated generation contains 35 percent of the population, it will literally knock our current health care delivery system (if "system" is the right word) on its ear. "Spending increases of 62 percent and 32 percent are projected for Medicare and Social Security over the next five years, compared to 14 percent for all other domestic programs combined" (Green, 1988). Conversely, Aid to Families with Dependent Children has declined by 35 percent since 1970. As the Baby Boomers head for their fifties and sixties, there will be additional expenditures and a radical departure from our high tech medical system with its marketplace mentality. The emphasis will be, even more decidedly, upon modifying unhealthy behaviors. Leisure will be the realm most affected by such changes. What people eat, drink, and smoke will be more carefully monitored. Employers will increasingly seek to shape the discretionary behavior of their employees.

An older society will change every facet of life: the food we eat, the ads we see on television, our literature, transportation systems, and, certainly, the way we use leisure. Public leisure service agencies, which have been disproportionately oriented toward the young (and toward males) will have to rethink what they are doing and why.

The Beginning of the Women's Revolution

While the status of women is in a process of transition, there is reason to believe that we are, essentially, in the first of three phases in this revolutionary process (Masnick and Banes, 1980). The first phase of change in women's roles has been entry into the labor force. Today, roughly six of ten women over the age of 21 work outside the home. Certainly there have been mixed reasons for this phenomenon. One important reason has been the desire to continue a family's material standard of living during periods of inflation and declines in the value of the dollar. Much of this employment, however, has been temporary or undertaken in episodes of a few years to "help out" with family finances. While this first phase has produced new conditions within the family, societal responses to these changes have been minimal. To a great extent, women who enter the labor force are "adding" a role rather than "changing" their role. Women still undertake an estimated four-fifths of household maintenance and child-rearing duties, although some changes are beginning to be evident in household division of labor.

The second phase of the change in women's roles, which is beginning to occur now, is attachment to careers. A career has a very different meaning from mere employment, since it implies special training, advancement to higher positions and, perhaps, the occupation becoming a more central part of one's self-definition. As women enter careers and experience advancement and many years of uninterrupted work, society will be changed in a number of ways to accommodate the situation. Licensed day care facilities, increased use of flexible working hours, paternity and maternity leave, job-sharing, and women in top positions within corporations are all likely to become more prevalent. Today, women constitute slightly over one-half of all full-time undergraduate students in colleges and universities and the mix of subjects they are studying is changing dramatically.

The third stage of the revolution in women's roles will be economic parity. Women will have the same earning power of men. This is when the real revolution will occur since our society empowers people who earn good incomes. Economic parity between the sexes will change almost every social institution, every form of behavior. It will raise more than token questions concerning who should fix meals, wash the car, or pay alimony. Economic parity will also cause society to begin exploring the more fundamental issue regarding women — how are women different from men and how can those differences be expressed and benefit society? As Simone de Beauvior has observed, the issues of equality are important to women but after such issues have been dealt with, however imperfectly, the larger issue of identity remains. Women and men are different. Their movement patterns are different while still in the womb. They react differently to a variety of stimuli at birth. They exhibit different forms of strength. Men and women are different and the emerging society will be one in which the uniqueness of women plays a more important part in shaping our social institutions. Leisure will be changed by women, first by increasing concern with equality and eventually with reshaping leisure resources to the unique interests and needs of women.

Perhaps an example is in order. At my university there is a huge football stadium, seating 85,000 people. It was built, essentially, to satisfy a leisure interest of males. As women's roles change there has been great concern about whether or not equal amounts of money are spent for varsity sports for women as are for men. While this is an important issue, the more important issue in the next few decades will be the process of determining what uniquenesses in women can be translated into forms of leisure expression which lead to something equivalent to but, perhaps, radically different from an 85,000 seat football stadium.

Living Above Our Means

Americans, both individually and collectively, are living above their economic means at an alarming rate. Perhaps a large part of the reason for this has been the mistaken belief that the period after World War II, during which we prospered economically due to the devastation of many countries which were our economic competitors, was attributable to our inherent superiority. Not only did we begin to expect more and more material goods, we also began to lose the sense of community and work ethic which contributed to our economic well being. Americans today save less than three percent of their pay, compared to 14 percent saved by the West Germans and 19 percent saved by the Japanese. Our Federal budget deficit runs between one and two hundred billion dollars per year and one dollar of every five in each year's Federal budget now goes to service the interest on the debt. The majority of federal spending is for entitlement programs which can't be changed unless legislation is changed removing some form of entitlements, such as Medicare, Aid to Dependent Families or the subsidy to homeowners in the form of tax write-offs of interest paid on mortgages. Most of these entitlement programs are, themselves, in need of additional funding. Medicare, for instance, will see its hospital trust fund go into debt in 1993 and provide annual deficits of $27 billion per year by the end of the 1990s without additional revenues.

America has gone from being the biggest creditor in the world to being the biggest debtor. Our foreign trade imbalance is increasingly serious. Compared to a decade ago, Americans are less well off economically. All this has happened in spite of the fact that we have the highest percentage of citizens in the labor force today than we have ever had. Add to this the need to replace bridges and highways in many states, the great expense which is looming to begin cleaning up the polluted water supply in most of the nation's major aquifers, the gradual decrease in the number of working people who support a single person on Social Security from five to three or even two, the potentially huge bill from the treatment of AIDS victims and drug addicts and others. The likelihood of increased dependence on foreign oil or a large rise in the cost of domestic oil multiplies the problem. At the present rate of use, all known oil reserves in the United States will be exhausted in 1996; "half the oil pumped out of the ground in 1986 came from countries that in the year 2000 will have no oil at all" (Brekke, 1988). The economic cost of the havoc that widespread drug use is creating further compounds the problem. Americans are responsible for an estimated 40 percent of all illegal drug use in the world (CNN, April 15, 1988). There is not a train wreck, plane crash, car wreck or death of a professional athlete which does not bring about the immediate question as to whether drugs are involved. Marijuana is the leading cash agricultural product in the United States.

The consequences of living above our means will be with us for many years. Taxes will have to go up and entitlements cut. Our military presence in the world will have to be reduced. We also have the potential for intergenerational conflict between young and old, the young blaming the old for living above its means, establishing retirement programs which cannot be duplicated for the young and federal debt which has been passed on for the young to try to deal with. During our leisure, the new economic constraints are likely to make us more planned, cautious in expenditures and critical of service.

Consuming More Than Our Share

North Americans have developed a style of life and an attitude toward the consumption of material goods which serves as a negative model for the rest of the world, rapes the world's resources and does untold environmental harm. Perhaps a few examples will suffice. The United States, which represents six percent of the world's population, consumes one-third of the earth's energy and one-ninth of all its oil (Lamm, 1985). Each American uses about two tons of wood each and every year. By comparison, those in developing nations each use, on average, only enough wood to produce two copies of the Sunday New York Times. United States citizens use twice as much paper per capita as the British or Japanese. We have the highest rate of automobile ownership in the world and, if that ownership rate were matched by the Chinese, an immediate ecological disaster would result. Our desire for cheap hamburger has led to the removal of tropical forests in Central America to produce rangeland for cattle. Two-thirds of the virgin forests of Central America are already gone.

The depletion of the ozone layer, contamination of water, from ground water to the oceans, the increasing damage done by acid rain in North America as well as much of Europe, the contamination of soil by pesticides, garbage and chemical dumping all present situations that attest to the necessity of change. It is the depletion of animal species, however, that is perhaps the most ominous indicator of the great trouble we are in. The current rate of the extinction of species may be 10,000 per year. In our lifetime, we could participate in the annihilation of one-fourth of the species which live on earth (Lamm, 1985). Not only does such a tragedy attest to the failure of our way of life, it may also jeopardize it, since genetic diversity is of fundamental importance to our planet's well being.

As our society has decentralized, the movement away from cities has resulted in urban development increasing much faster

than population growth. In the geographic region surrounding
New York City, for example, in the last two decades

> the population in the 31 counties in the region rose
> just 5 percent, while developed land, including
> roads, developed one-third. Unprotected and un-
> developed land declined to 60 percent from 72
> percent of total. Protected open space increased
> to 11 percent from 6. In the next three decades,
> Regional Plan projects a 25 percent increase in de-
> veloped land (New York Times, Feb. 4, 1988).

Similar situations exist in many other locations. The
staggering growth of traffic is linked to this urban development.
"While the population is expanding at about one percent a year, the
number of vehicles and total miles traveled have risen four to six
times faster..." (Dentzer, 1988). Much of this increase has come in
the suburbs, where almost half the population lives and businesses
are relocating. Certainly such problems impact directly upon our
natural resources used for recreation. An estimated 171 National
Park Service sites, for instance, are presently under threat from
such development. The borders of parks or conservation areas at
all levels are increasingly subject to such problems and the air and
water within these sites is not exempt from pollution. The idea
that land can be "preserved," in effect stored away from the problems of the world, is increasingly suspect.

The response to the previous indicators of the fundamental
ecological problems we face is, increasingly, divided into two
distinct types of responses, each of which reflect differing views of
reality. One view is that nature must be conquered and artificial
environments developed, the other that we must learn to "fit in"
with nature, causing the least possible disturbance to the natural
environment.

Taking Ourselves Seriously — Narcissism and Fitness

The last decade has been characterized by increasing self-absorption. It would appear that we take ourselves far more seriously than ever before and worry more about who we are, how we look, whether we are happy and whether we are healthy. While a number of theories have been advanced to explain this situation, Lasch (1979) argued persuasively that our current narcissism could be attributed to:

> a way of life that is dying — the culture of competitive individualism, which in its decadence has carried the logic of individualism to the extreme of a war of all against all, the pursuit of happiness to the dead end of a narcissistic preoccupation with the self. Strategies of narcissistic survival now present themselves as emancipation from the repressive conditions of the past, thus giving rise to a cultural revolution that reproduces the worst features of the collapsing civilization it claims to criticize (Lasch, 1979).

Individualism, in short, while coming to an end, has produced a revolution (probably short lived) in our culture in which selfishness is the rule. Our sense of community has broken down. Our individual sense of obligation to others has stretched thin, our sense of history has almost disappeared, our primary responsibility is not to family, religion, state or posterity, but to ourselves.

> The new narcissist is haunted not by guilt but by anxiety. He seeks not to inflict his own certainties on others but to find a meaning in life. Liberated from the superstitions of the past, he doubts even the reality of his own existence. Superficially

relaxed and tolerant, he finds little use for dogmas
of racial and ethnic purity but at the same time for-
feits the security of group loyalties and regards
everyone as a rival for the favors conferred by a
paternalistic state. His sexual attitudes are permissive rather than puritanical even though his emanci-
pation from ancient taboos brings him no sexual
peace. Fiercely competitive in his demand for
approval and acclaim, he distrusts competition
because he associates it unconsciously with an
unbridled urge to destroy (Lasch, 1979).

The narcissist, according to Lasch, praises respect for rules
but secretly feels they do not apply to him, praises teamwork but
has deep antisocial feelings, will acquire material goods endlessly
but not for future gain; only for immediate gratification.

Certainly the culture of narcissism has been encouraged by
the content of the huge amount of advertising we are exposed to,
encouraging us to buy impulsively, to be self-conscious and to live
in the present.

Narcissism has meant that play, like work, is to be taken
seriously. In the emergence of what Wolfenstein (1955) referred
to as a "fun morality," people wonder if they are doing as well as
they should, not just at work, but also at play.

In today's society, where impulse rather than calculation is
the determinant of human conduct and where society is held
responsible for the problems of the individual, a "government-
oriented" professional class has sprung up and, like capitalists, has
sought to generate a demand for its own services (Moynihan,
1976). New demands and new sources of discontent must be
generated which can be made better through the provision of
services just as the capitalist claims to make people better through
the acquisition of material goods. In both cases, a therapeutic
approach is taken. Since society is to blame for the problems of
individuals, the individual needs to be restored to wholeness
through the acquisition of a variety of products or services.

The behaviors involved in using these products or services then become a means to an end. Less and less behavior is undertaken for its own sake and even behavior which was its own justification, such as writing poetry, now becomes justified as a means to an end — "poetry therapy." To a remarkable extent, this mentality characterizes much of what we do in everyday life. The idea of evil becomes obsolete and the idea of self-improvement to make up for the problems society has imposed on the individual becomes all important.

No where is narcissism and taking ourselves seriously more evident than in regard to "physical fitness." Much of our concern with "fitness" is more accurately concern for a beautiful body. Much of our sport participation appears to be part of the "all against all" struggle which Lasch mentioned. Much of the exercise phenomenon appears to be part of the therapeutic approach to life, in which new problems are perpetually discovered to be overcome through new forms of human movement.

Certainly there are many reasons for the alleged rise in exercise and sport participation. Many are health related. Some are related to finance, since unhealthy individuals cost both employers and insurance companies money. Also, sport participation and exercise may reflect higher levels of education and greater awareness of the benefits of exercise.

Many of these same reasons apply to the increase in interest in diet and attempts at healthy eating. Our obsession with how much we weigh and what we eat and drink has led to many changes in our diet and the preparation of food. A "health food" industry has sprung up and consumption of red meat has declined. Nonetheless, as with physical exercise, in spite of recent changes there is reason to believe that Americans don't necessarily translate their increased concern about fitness and diet, as well as their increased knowledge, into action.

> Several independent polls of American health and
> eating habits recently showed that the extensive
> publicity on these issues is having little effect on

> lifestyles. Many people say (and probably believe)
> they're changing their eating and exercise habits
> for the better, but it could be they've just figured
> out the right things to say on surveys. The fact is,
> their habits are pretty much the same. Or getting
> worse (Blake Weisenthal, 1988).

Perhaps a few examples will suffice. One federal government survey showed that, on a given day, 77 percent of Americans eat white bread, 40 percent consume cookies, soft drinks and whole milk, 30 percent eat hot dogs and luncheon meats, while only 18 percent eat broccoli and other cruciferous vegetables which have been shown to inhibit cancer growth. More than four out of ten eat no fruit at all. A New York Times survey showed that "People between eighteen and twenty-nine years old . . . have the least wholesome eating and exercise habits, preferring beef, sweets, salty and fried foods over all others and exercising less often than people over the age of 64" (New York Times quoted by Blake Weisenthal, 1988). Similarly, a 1988 Louis Harris poll found that only 42 percent of adults surveyed said they made any attempt to limit their intake of high cholesterol foods. That figure is down from 1987, when 46 percent sought to limit such intake (Louis Harris quoted by Blake Weisenthal, 1988).

It is actually extremely difficult to determine if exercise has increased or not within the last decade, although the prevailing belief is that it has. Certainly the belief in the importance of exercise has increased. Certainly, too, there is a section of the public who exercise regularly. For example, when considering only those who participate at least 100 days a year or more, there are still 10.3 million Americans who walk for fitness, 8.1 million who run or jog, 4.9 million who bicycle and 2.6 million who swim.

Perhaps it can be said that individuals in our society, in taking themselves more seriously, have more individual concern about health and fitness, but such concern is only partially expressed by our actual behavior. Individual concern abut health does not yet appear to include concern for the health of others.

Leisure As the Emerging Center of the Economy

To a remarkable extent, leisure behavior has pushed its way to the center of our economy. It is difficult, of course, to accurately measure leisure monetary spending. Some leisure behaviors are illegal, such as many forms of gambling, which generated an estimated 5.2 billion dollars in 1984 (Gaming and Wagering Business Magazine, 1986). Other forms of spending have a leisure component and a non-leisure component, such as the purchase of a sports car which is used to drive to work as well as for pleasure driving or racing. There are also huge hidden costs such as "business entertainment" which often have a strong leisure component. In spite of this, products and services used during leisure have become a critical variable in our economy.

There is every indication that leisure has become the primary economic base for many large cities. While cities traditionally have been created around manufacturing, their economies are being transformed in such a way that they are increasingly dependent upon a variety of forms of leisure expression. A great deal of decentralization has taken place both in manufacturing and in the service industries — almost anything can be produced almost anywhere. As the industrial base of cities has eroded, much of their economic well-being is dependent upon diverse forms of leisure expression. Such forms of expression can be seen in urban waterfront redevelopment, as well as more emphasis upon and competition for conventions, tourism, shopping, sport, entertainment, dining and drinking, historic preservation, festivals and celebrations, non-vocational adult education and the fine arts.

While Americans are becoming more cautious and critical consumers in regard to leisure expenditures, the increases in leisure spending from 1975 to 1985 are as follows: toys and sports supplies from $8.9 billion to $20.6 billion; magazines and newspapers from $6.3 billion to $13.3 billion; flowers, seeds and potted plants from $2.6 billion to $5.5 billion; boats from $2.1 billion to $5.9

billion; spectator sports from $1.3 billion to $2.8 billion; and cable TV from $0.7 billion to $8.6 billion (U.S. Department of Commerce, 1986). The list can go on and on. Surely also if many forms of drug use are considered to be leisure, spending has sky-rocketed.

It is clear that travel and tourism account for increasing amounts of spending in the United States as well as many other countries. Total travel spending in the United States increased from approximately $94 billion in 1975 to $259 billion in 1985. Of this $259 billion, about $36 billion was spent on transportation, $42 billion on lodging, $132 billion on eating and drinking, and $49 billion on entertainment and recreation (U.S. Travel Data Center, 1988). Americans spent about $17 billion on overseas travel in 1985 while foreign visitors spent about $12 billion in the United States (U.S. Department of Commerce, 1986). As the dollar has been recently devalued against other currencies, the amount of overseas spending in the United States has doubtlessly increased.

The extent to which Americans travel to other countries has increased for a variety of reasons, including cheaper airfares, greater national-level tourism promotion efforts and, perhaps, greater interest in other countries due to higher education levels and more economic interdependency. In 1985 a large study of American pleasure travel undertaken by Tourism Canada found that 21 percent of the American public had visited Canada for a vacation or pleasure trip during the last three years, eight percent had similarly visited the Caribbean, eight percent had visited Europe and 13 percent had visited Mexico. Such totals indicate that foreign travel for pleasure has become a relatively common occurrence within our society.

Tourism, according to most tourism experts, either is or will become the largest industry in the world within the next decade. Its impacts, financial, ecological and social, will be enormous.

A Society With More But Not Better Education

While our society is characterized by increasing years of formal education, the changing nature of that education has been such that many Americans are scientifically illiterate. Our formal education levels have risen dramatically from 1940 to 1985. The proportion of the population with high school diplomas tripled during that period while the proportion of American adults ages 25 and over who graduated from colleges and universities quadrupled (U.S. Census Bureau, 1987). By 1985, the proportion of adults age 25 and over who have completed high school had risen from 24 percent to 74 percent. Similarly, those who have four or more years of college have increased from five percent to 19 percent of the population. Nearly half of all high school graduates attend college and slightly more than one-half of them complete four years of college. While the gap between blacks and whites is closing in terms of high school graduation, the percentage of blacks enrolled in colleges and universities has actually fallen. Among 18- to 24-year-old blacks who have graduated from high school, the percentage enrolled in colleges fell from 33.5 in 1976 to 26.1 in 1985. In general, however, more years of formal education is a pronounced trend in our society.

There is increasing evidence that, in spite of higher level of formal education, Americans are learning significantly less about math and science than students in other industrialized nations. We are simply not keeping up with the rest of the industrialized world as students. A soon to be released study by the International Association for the Evaluation of Education Achievement will demonstrate how far American students are behind. Preliminary findings show that American fifth graders rank eighth among 15 nations in math and science achievement and that the lowest 25 percent of United States student are "scientifically illiterate" (Beck, 1987). American high school students test lower in math than their peers in 18 other industrialized nations. Our seniors who take second-year biology courses finished dead last in international comparisons. There is other evidence of our demise in science and math. In 1986, 60 percent of all doctoral degrees in engineering went to students from foreign countries. Almost one-half of all patents awarded by the U.S. Patent and Trademark Office went to inventors from other countries. The evidence is overwhelming of our current inability to compete with the rest of the modern world. Thus, a dangerous situation has evolved. More and more students graduate from college, having developed high expectations about the quality of life they expect to lead, high levels of expectation concerning compensation and satisfaction from employment, high levels of exposure to a wide variety of leisure behaviors, but comparatively little training in the subjects which have led to the advancement of technology. The question must be asked whether this situation will signal the decline of the United States as a leader in technology. It may be more accurate to say that it already has.

Increasingly, the changes which took place in colleges and universities during the 1960s are blamed for the demise in the quality of higher education in the U.S. Consider the following comments from Allan Bloom (1987):

> About the sixties it is now fashionable to say that although there were indeed excesses, many good things resulted. But, so far as universities were concerned, I know of nothing positive coming from that period; it was an unmitigated disaster for them. I hear that the good things were "greater openness," "less rigidity," "freedom from authority," etc. — but these have no content and express no view of what is wanted from a university education.

Elsewhere he wrote:

> The reforms were without content, made for the "inner-directed" person. They were an acquiescence

in a leveling off of the peaks and were the source of
the collapse of the entire American educational
structure, recognized by all parties when they talk
about the need to go "back to basics." This collapse
is directly traceable to both the teachings and the
deeds of the universities in the sixties. More important than the bad teachers and the self-indulgent
doctrines was the disappearance of the reasons for
the models of — for example — "the King's English."
The awareness of the highest is what points the
lowest upward. Now, it may be possible, with a lot
of effort and political struggle, to return to earlier
standards of accomplishment in the three R's, but
it will not be so easy to recover the knowledge of
philosophy, history and literature that was trashed
(Bloom, 1987).

While many may not agree with Bloom's assessment, it
seems fair to say that universities, perhaps with good intentions,
have nevertheless failed to provide intellectual leadership in a
mistaken attempt to gain popularity with those who were ignorant
of their historic mission.

A More Addicted Society

America is in the middle of a crisis concerning drug use. An estimated 40 percent of the world's illegal drugs are used by Americans (CNN, April 15, 1988). Thus drugs have become yet one more resource of which Americans use far more than their share. More than 10 percent of Americans regularly use illegal drugs, costing an estimated $33 billion in lost working time and an unbelievable amount of crime (Curtiss, 1987). A 12 city study showed that 53 to 79 percent of men arrested for serious crimes were drug users. About three out of four cities have a seven-week waiting list of those seeking treatment for drug problems. Illegal drug sales have become a major industry for organized crime, from youth gangs to the Mafia.

In understanding the phenomenon of addiction in our society, it is important to understand what addiction is. According to a leading researcher on addiction, Stanton Peele (1978) "The definitive characteristic of every sort of addiction is that the addict regularly takes something that relieves some kind of pain." What the addict takes, or does, however, to relieve that pain varies widely. According to Peele, we cannot say that a given drug is addictive, since addiction is not a peculiar characteristic of drugs. Research shows compulsive addictive involvement in sexual behavior, gambling, eating, television viewing, running and other forms of behavior which may be thought of as "discretionary." Furthermore, these compulsions, such as compulsive eating, show all the signs of ritual, instant gratification, cultural variation and destruction of self-respect which drug addiction does. There is, additionally, great individual and cultural variation in the extent to which use of a given drug becomes addictive. More than 90 percent of U.S. soldiers in Viet Nam for whom heroin use was detected were able to give up the habit when back in the United States. One generation of Chinese society was devastated by opium use while other opium-using countries, such as India, underwent no such disaster. Some individuals report feeling instantly addicted to heroin after the first use while others, after years of daily use, quit with no withdrawal symptoms. The addictive personality is likely to accept magic solutions, and to suffer anxiety brought about by a discrepancy between society's values and personal lack of opportunity and lack of self-reliance. There is also great individual variation in the pharmacological action of drugs and in the ways in which various individuals metabolize chemicals, but these alone do not determine whether a person will become addicted (Peele, 1978).

Addiction, in summary, will not be removed from society by getting rid of all the supply of a certain drug, even if this could be accomplished. It is a pathological process of pain relief which involves many kinds of drug and non-drug behavior. Addiction is a "process rather than a condition" (Peele, 1978). It is a continuum rather than an all or nothing condition. The biggest addictions in our culture would appear to be the use of alcohol, nicotine, eating, prescription drugs and, perhaps, sexual behavior.

We may change our attitudes toward addiction within the next decade. Many futurists believe drugs will be decriminalized and will be treated as a controlled substance by the state. Law enforcement appears to have little effect on drug use, since one person in 10 in our society is a regular drug user. Legalizing drugs would drastically reduce crime since one-half or more of all crime is drug related. Further, the spread of AIDS would be reduced since intravenous drug users are currently the most at-risk population. The use of shared hypodermic needles is directly related to the fact that drug use is illegal. Also there would be a huge benefit for addicts if they could receive predictable quantities of the drug to which they are addicted and could re-enter the labor force. The occupation of many addicts now is theft, prostitution or other forms of crime made necessary by the addiction. A huge education program will also be necessary but one which is based on the understanding that addiction occurs when an individual seeks relief from pain. As a society, we must begin to understand and earnestly seek to do something about the source or sources of such pain.

The Rapidly Changing American Household and Family

The average U.S. household has changed dramatically in its composition and size during the last few decades and will continue to change. These changes will reshape our daily life and our leisure. In 1910 the average household consisted of 4.5 persons; that number has now shrunk to 2.64 and will continue to decline (U. S. Census Bureau, 1988). There has been a remarkable consistency in household size historically. In Britain, for example, the mean household size was 4.18 for the seventeenth century, 4.57 for the eighteenth century, and 4.21 for the nineteenth century (Pollock, 1987). While the myth may have been that huge extended families lived together, the reality was quite different. Households averaged between four and five residents for several centuries until the abrupt drop in the last few decades. Today, not only is household size declining, but we are witnessing basic changes in the composition of our households. Non-family households account for about one-fourth of all households and will approach 30 percent by 1995. These households consist primarily of young people not yet married, persons between marriages and, most often, the elderly. The traditional model of the Baby Boom Generation nuclear family, a father who works, a mother who serves as homemaker and children living at home, accounts for less than one out of five U.S. households. About one household in five has only one occupant and another 13 percent are single parent households. While households continue to get smaller and smaller, the rate of shrinkage is being slowed down somewhat by young people choosing, or being forced to remain at home. Four years after high school, 42 percent of the class of 1980 were single and living with parents compared with 25 percent of the class of 1972 (Better Homes and Gardens, 1988). The paychecks of 1980 graduates average 23 percent less than those of the class of 1972, after adjusting for inflation.

Changes in the American household reflect not only changes in the age structure of our society, but changes in our styles of living. "The contemporary increase in diversity of adult lifestyles — more single and gay couples, more divorce and family reconstitution (occurring at increasing rates even in later life) — points to a future of increasingly varied lifestyles and increasingly complex family roles as these individuals move into later life" (Sussman, 1985). Family and personal relations will be more diverse, less institutionalized and less predictable than at any other time during this century. These changes "will mean a reduction in both the power and the clarity of the norms prescribing how family members are to relate to one another" (Bengston and Dannefer, 1987). Certainly the use of leisure within these diverse kinds of families will play a central role in determining what new norms are created.

Intergenerational issues in family life will become more complex as four or five living generations within a family will no longer be remarkable. This will produce more "vertical" family relationships and, combined with higher divorce rates, mean that relations exist, for example, between a child and the father of their mother's third husband, for which we don't even have labels. It may also mean that those who are retired will increasingly take care of their parents.

Intergenerational relations are likely to become more intense, involving both greater cohesion and tension (Bengston and Dannefer, 1987). A decline in the number of children born per woman from 3.2 for women born in 1933 to 1.9 for women born in 1950 means that grandparents and parents will have fewer children with whom to interact.

While these relations may be more intense, "interfamilialties, based on religious, neighborhood or other forms of association, may to some extent serve as family surrogates and thus reduce the intrafamilial intensity" (Bengston and Dannefer, 1987). Leisure services may play an increasingly important role in bringing about and strengthening such ties.

Since analyses of family life among ethnic minorities reveal that economic deprivation and the dependence of one generation upon another are bases upon which family life has been organized for decades (Jackson, 1986), such minorities may cope better than those who experience it for the first time. Similarly, women who experienced deprivation during the Great Depression appeared to cope better with the adversities of age.

All of these changes in family life will bring about a rapid consideration of alternative responses. Currently the United States is the only industrialized nation other than South Africa without national health insurance. This is likely to change. Tax incentives which encourage job exploration may be considered as may a move to cut Social Security benefits or otherwise increase the tax obligation of well-to-do elderly.

Best (1980) and others have found a preference among many to rearrange the existing life course so that some "retirement" leisure time is transferred to the middle years, some "work" transferred to later life and some "education" spread over the entire life course. This breakup of the standardized life course is already beginning to happen and, as it intensifies, it will produce profound changes in the significance of age, and intergenerational relations. This will, in turn, produce changes in all of our social institutions, including leisure services, which are organized by making common assumptions about those in a particular age group or life stage.

The Changing Face of Crime

America has always been a violent culture. Our history attests to this as the following passage from Carl Sagan (1988) documents.

> The United States, founded on principles of freedom and liberty, was the last major nation to end chattel slavery; many of its founding fathers — George Washington and Thomas Jefferson among them — were slave owners; and racism was legally protected for a century after the slaves were freed. The United States has systematically violated more than 300 treaties it signed guaranteeing some of the rights of the original inhabitants of the country. In 1899, two years after becoming president, Theodore Roosevelt, in a widely admired speech, advocated "righteous war" as the sole means of achieving "national greatness." The United States invaded the Soviet Union in 1918 in an unsuccessful attempt to undo the Bolshevik Revolution. The United States invented nuclear arms and was the first and only nation to explode them against civilian populations, killing hundreds of thousands of men, women and children in the process. The United States had operational plans for the nuclear annihilation of the Soviet Union before there even was a Soviet nuclear weapon, and it has been the chief innovator in the continuing arms race.

Further, Sagan pointed out, our foreign policy has been filled with inconsistencies. We have opposed some regimes as terrorist while supporting South Africa and Chile, where citizens have almost no rights, sold arms to Iran while warning others not to, mined harbors in Nicaragua while expressing outrage at the Iranian mining of the Persian Gulf. We denounced Libya for killing children and, in return, killed their children in bombing raids. We are one of the top two arms merchants in the world, sometimes supplying both sides of a conflict.

America, in summary, has been and continues to be a violent culture. Part of the reason for this is the widespread owner- ship of handguns. We have the highest rate of such ownership of any nation. It may be coincidence that last year there were more murders in Detroit than in Britain, but it is a fact.

To a great extent, fear of crime shapes the choices of individuals during leisure and represents a significant constraint on our individual freedom. Nearly one-half of the residents of large cities have altered their lifestyles because of fear of crime (Bennett, 1988). What we particularly fear, of course, is violent crime, and most violent crime is committed by young males be- tween the ages of 15-25. Drug use, as mentioned previously, is also associated with a large percentage of many types of crime, particularly theft by those who need money to continue using an illegal drug. Arrest rates reach a high at around 18 years of age for such males, who tend to be poor and uneducated, and then decline dramatically. As this age group declines as a portion of our popu- lation, we are likely to see less street crime but, as crime expert Georgette Bennett (1988) warned us, we are likely to have increased white collar crime.

Perhaps because our concern with violent crime and the attention it receives in the mass media, the following recent trends are surprising. Victimization rates have declined by 16 percent since 1981 and only 10 percent of all victimizations are violent crimes. Older people are the least frequent victims of street crime; young people the most. Men are twice as likely to be victims of street crime as women; blacks almost twice as likely as whites. Violent crimes have dropped in schools by nearly two-fifths since 1973. Banks lose eight times more money to employees, execu- tives and swindlers than to street criminals. The likelihood of being in a car crash is 32 times greater than being the victim of a serious assault (Bennett, 1988).

Given the changing demographic composition of society, Bennett (1988) predicted a number of major changes in the type and extent of crime in our country. Street crime will decrease greatly as will violence, although a small percentage of youth will actually become more violent. Higher crime rates will shift from the Frostbelt to the Sunbelt and from cities to suburbs and rural areas. So-called white collar crime will increase greatly, particularly computer crime, pension abuse, real estate and construction industry corruption spurred by a building glut, and other high tech crime.

Most consensual crime, Bennett believed, such as drug abuse, homosexual behavior, prostitution, and gambling will be legalized. While drug use may be legalized, she believed, it will decline. Drug use, as a number of experts have argued, simply doesn't fit with the rest of society's agenda, such as preventive health, fitness, body consciousness, economic cutbacks and a demanding work schedule. In many of these matters, law has very little impact on behavior. In fact, there is a tendency to overestimate the extent to which law enforcement is related to crime. Of the total criminal offenses known to police between 1972 and 1983, only about one in five resulted in arrest (U.S. Department of Justice, 1972-1983). When you consider the large number of crimes that are never reported and the large number of arrests which do not result in conviction, the relation between crime and police is extremely weak.

In the future, Bennett (1988) believed, we will rely more and more on self-policing as the main means of crime control. Additionally, the criminal justice system will be managed, increasingly, by private police, private courts, private prisons and private probation systems. There may also be increasing use of confinement techniques in sentencing criminals, in effect imprisoning them in their homes, with the help of electronic monitoring devices, rather than sending them to overcrowded, ineffective and incredibly expensive prisons.

All of these changes indicate that crime will change in nature, be responded to in new ways and that our definition of

what constitutes a crime will change. Certainly there is considerable evidence that our current system of crime prevention and
criminal justice is a failure in terms of deterring crime, convicting
criminals and rehabilitating criminals. Additionally, the system is
extraordinarily expensive to administer and favors the wealthy in
each step of the process.

Increased Inequality

During the last decade, America has been increasingly split into a country of haves and have nots. This has occurred not only because of changes in our economic competitiveness within an emerging world economy, but also because of conscious political choice. Our distribution of wealth more and more resembles a developing nation rather than one which was formerly known for its huge middle class. The evidence of such change is indisputable. Most households have seen a decline or leveling off of income during the last 10 years. Average family income reached $24,184 in 1977 and has not changed much since. (See Table 1).

Table 1
Average After-Tax Family Income
(in 1987 dollars)

Income group by deciles	1977 average income	1988 average income	% change	Dollar + or -
First	$3,528	$3,157	-10.5%	- $371
Second	$7,084	$6,990	-1.3%	- $94
Third	$10,740	$10,614	-1.2%	- $126
Fourth	$14,323	$14,266	-0.4%	- $57
Fifth	$18,043	$18,076	+0.2%	+ $33
Sixth	$22,009	$22,259	+1.1%	+ $250
Seventh	$26,240	$27,038	+3.0%	+ $798
Eighth	$31,568	$33,282	+5.4%	+ $1,714
Ninth	$39,236	$42,323	+7.9%	+ $3,087
Tenth	$70,459	$89,783	+27.4%	+ $19,324
Top 5%	$90,756	$124,651	+37.3%	+ $33,895
Top 1%	$174,498	$303,900	+74.2%	+ $129,402
All groups	$24,184	$26,494	+9.6%	+ $2,310

Source: Congressional Budget Office

In spite of this stagnation, during the last 10 years, "The top twentieth of the population has seen average family income grow by $33, 895 and the top hundredth (those now earning more than $303,900) by $129,402" (Edsall, 1988). An increase of married women in the labor force has not affected the widening gap between rich and poor, since the various effects of working married women "simply cancelled each other out" (Budd, 1987). The after-tax family income of those in the lowest tenth in our society is, on average, over 10 percent less than their income from 1977 to 1988 while those in the top tenth have gained more than 27 percent. Those whose family incomes are in the top one percent have had an extraordinary 74.2 percent increase. When these statistics are combined with the fact that the share of federal dollars spent on education, training, employment, social services, health, income security, and housing has dropped from 23.5 percent in 1980 to 18.3 in 1987, it is apparent that the loss of those in lower income levels has been even greater than the table reveals. Finally, when we add the fact that the percentage of the budget spent on the military during this period increased from 22.7 percent to 28.4 percent, in spite of being at peace, our priorities are apparent.

The political groundwork for this remarkable split in the economic well-being of our society has been accomplished, according to Edsall (1988), through a number of circumstances, including the shift in jobs from manufacturing to services and the accompanying decline in union membership from 23 percent to 17 percent of all workers, the rise of political-action committees (PACS) which now supply 36 percent of the total cost of political campaigns in the U.S. House of Representatives, the erosion of urban voting strength, the increasing need for huge amounts of money to run political campaigns and the ability of the wealthy to respond to and shape this process, and, finally, the lack of awareness of the public concerning the new inequality and its causes.

> The new inequality . . . is intrinsically invisible.
> People may sense that they are losing power; many
> know that they are losing money. But the extent of

their loss becomes apparent only in statistical comparisons. The three-fifths of the population exper-
iencing little or no gain in after tax income is not
angry at the top twentieth. Those on the losing end
aren't demanding remedies, because they aren't
aware that there is a collective problem (Edsall, 1988).

Perhaps part of the reason for this lack of awareness is that
the public has had an extremely personable man as its President
who initiated such policies. Perhaps, too, there was the belief that
"supply-side" economics would trickle down wealth for all. Additionally, revulsion with big government and taxes, which led to the
"tax revolt," laid the groundwork for the feeling that people should
return to some model of self-sufficiency. Unfortunately, this
occurred at the very time when our population was becoming less
self-sufficient. Unfortunately, too, this movement did not cut
federal spending; it merely resulted in a transfer from social services to the military and welfare for the wealthy.

The impact of the increasing gap between rich and poor on
leisure behavior is certainly complex. On the one hand, it appears
to have led to the use of leisure for the conspicuous display of
wealth. It has also, as mentioned elsewhere, brought about a
decline in the amount of time spent in leisure for many who are
scrambling to maintain their material standard of living. Those
who provide leisure services have, increasingly, targeted their
services at those with specific economic situations. Market seg-
mentation has occurred more rapidly as the life circumstances of
the population have been increasingly differentiated.

The Plight of Children

As some of the previous discussion suggests, children are the most "at risk" age group in our society. The following statistics, reported by Congressman George Miller, Chair of the U.S. House Select Committee on Children, Youth and Families, provides detail concerning the plight of America's four-and five-year-olds: one-in-four children is poor (two-in-four if Hispanic, even more if black), one-in-six has no health insurance, one-in-seven may drop out of school, one-in-five may become a teen-age parent, one-in-four will spend time on welfare (Miller, 1988). The United States today ranks seventh in life expectancy, tenth in educational expenditure per student, tenth in public health expenditures, seventeenth in infant mortality, and twenty-second in population per physician.

Today 25 percent of babies born are born to mothers who received no first trimester prenatal care. For black mothers, this figure is 40 percent. Over 25 percent of children age one to four were not inoculated against one or more serious childhood diseases such as polio or mumps. Less than 20 percent of eligible children participate in Head Start programs, 40 percent of increasingly prevalent low birthweight infants die during the first year of birth and many who survive are developmentally disabled.

The role call of depressing statistics can go on and on. Children appear to be less physically fit than were their predecessors, they are frequently physically abused, and millions are "latch-key children" who are home alone after school. It is, then, not surprising that a recent study found that, of the 54.5 percent of the U.S. households which have a VCR, youngsters under 18 spend twice as much time watching taped programs as do adults (Associated Press, 1988). Indeed, a study by the Institute for Social Research found that "one activity dominates the American family's time together; watching television. No other single activity consumes as much free time" (Institute for Social Research, 1986). Children with employed mothers spent an average of six hours and forty minutes per week watching TV with one or both parents while children of full-time homemaker mothers spent even more time watching with one or both parents — eight hours and eight minutes. The total time children spent each week watching TV with or without their parents was 14 hours and 49 minutes per week for children of employed mothers and 16 hours and 13 minutes for children of homemakers. While we should interpret such figures with caution (some studies show that no one is in the room for up to one-third of the time that a television is on), it would appear that television is playing a major role in babysitting children and, literally, in raising them.

Children's use of leisure may be related to what they learn and their success in school. A major study of high school students undertaken by the U.S. Department of Education found that students who are active in extra-curricular activities tend to get good grades (Connell, 1988). Those who participated in four or more activities had much better grades than average.

While it is difficult to pinpoint all the factors which contribute to the plight of children, perhaps the most important one has been a basic change in family living patterns, due to both dramatically higher divorce rates and entry of mothers into the labor force at the very time that the Federal Government greatly lessened its concern and economic support for children in favor of other spending priorities, such as the military. Perhaps because of this, children are more likely to live below the poverty line than the elderly. (See Figure 2).

This basic disjuncture between the changing realities of the American family and government policy has meant that many children are, increasingly, raising themselves. The evidence is, historically, that children who are forced to raise themselves are not able to accomplish this extraordinarily difficult task without incurring severe, lingering problems. As a nation we are simply not prepared for the large scale entry of women into the labor force, nor are we prepared for the reductions in material standard of living which would have allowed families to have only one full-time or perhaps two part-time workers.

Figure 2
Percentage of Elderly and Children
Living Below Poverty Level

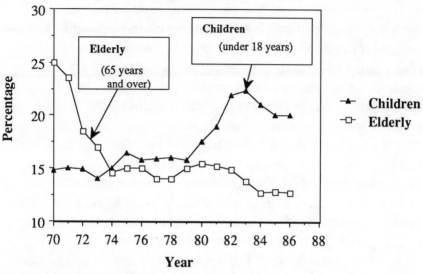

Source: Census Bureau

It may also be argued that the emphasis upon individual fulfillment and the emergent culture of narcissism, discussed elsewhere, has been a contributing factor to the plight of children. Raising children is hard work which requires the sacrifice or deferral of many individual desires. There seems to be evidence that the willingness to make such sacrifices has been lessened.

A Changing Job Market

While those in the Baby Boom Generation have been raised with expectations concerning work which are higher than those of any previous generation, these expectations will have to be tempered. The ideas that seniority on the job automatically brings increasing rewards, the expectation of continuous prosperity and the belief that work will be both extrinsically and intrinsically rewarding will all be subject to question.

A number of reasons will reshape such job expectations. As mentioned elsewhere, our national debt and changing competitive position in world markets make continuing economic prosperity questionable. Additionally, our labor market, during the last decade, has become one where there are "too many chiefs and not enough braves" (Jones, 1980). A recent estimate of the growth of middle and upper management in the United States over the next several years was 21 percent, while the pool of employees expecting to move into such positions will grow by 42 percent (Dannefer, 1983). Actually, middle and upper management positions may be cut drastically from what exist now to make U.S. companies more competitive with other countries (Peters, 1987).

While the absolute number of jobs has increased during the last two decades, the majority of these jobs have been low paying, high rotation, dead end positions. A projection made by the U.S. Bureau of Labor Statistics from 1978 to 1990 (Carey, 1981) identified the following positions as being those where the largest number of new jobs would be created: (1) janitors, (2) nurses' aides and orderlies, (3) sales clerks, (4) cashiers, (5) waiters and waitresses, (6) general office clerks, (7) professional nurses, and (8) fast food workers. Such occupations were projected to account for nearly 4.5 million new jobs over this 12 year period. While "high tech" positions such as computer systems analysts, operators and programmers have had the fastest growth rates, these three occupations have created fewer than 500,000 new jobs during the same period.

Although much has been made of the "Yuppies," a recent analysis revealed only five percent of the Baby Boom Generation qualified for this designation (making at least $39,000 per year). Seventy-two percent of the Baby Boom cohort work in the types of low-paying service jobs previously described averaging about $10,000 a year (Kim, in press, quoted by Bengston and Dannefer, 1987). These figures indicate that the members of the Baby Boom Generation "collectively face a disastrous retirement" (Hewitt, 1986). At the same time such workers will be taxed more heavily for pension and Social Security plans, their lifetime earnings will decline. In particular, many fewer of this generation will experience the kind of peak in earnings in their forties to sixties that most male labor force participants in preceding generations enjoyed (Bengston and Dannefer, 1987).

These changes will have immediate effects on how people live. Owning a house, for instance, will continue to become increasingly rare. (See Table 2). The proportion of the paycheck used to make mortgage payments was less than one-fourth of household income in 1973 but today approaches one-half.

Table 2
Percent Owning Homes, By Age

	25-29	35-39	45-49
1979	44%	70%	77%
1981	41%	69%	76%
1983	38%	66%	75%
1985	37%	65%	74%
1987	36%	64%	75%

Source: U.S. Census Bureau

In summary, "the old of the twenty-first century will be the largest, and perhaps initially the healthiest, older population in the nation's history. However, they may also be markedly less well off, than, say, persons entering old age today" (Bengston and Dannefer, 1987).

Another negative aspect of the change in kinds of jobs held is that the "de-skilling" of the labor force, the increasingly fragmented, mechanized, automated, bureaucratized and regimented nature of many jobs, may also be associated with mental and psychological loss. The resourcefulness and creativity of individuals may suffer. If the opportunity to exercise complex skills and activity routines declines at work, the ability to do so in other areas of life, such as leisure, may also decline.

Other changes in the labor force and conditions of labor have been identified by the U.S. Department of Labor (1988) as follows: a shrinking pool of younger workers entering the labor force, one out of five of whom will be minority group members; an increase in the average age of workers to 39 by the year 2000, rapid turnover and change in industries requiring some workers to change jobs five or six times during their lifetime; international competition leading to the need for higher levels of analytic skills among workers to remain competitive; a labor force in which 47 percent of the workers are women; a tight labor market in which employers are faced with skill shortages, leading to exporting jobs overseas, higher wages for qualified workers, automation investment and spending more for training and education of workers. Work will be done, in summary, by older workers who will need higher levels of skill and more flexibility in the way they live.

Longer range predictions about jobs are often more optimistic. John Diebold (1987), an authority on technology and management, believed that jobs dealing with health care, information services, travel and leisure, training, consulting and teaching will become more abundant. The impact of job on one's self-definition, Diebold believed, will be less than today, with leisure activities becoming a more important basis upon which people are judged by others and judge themselves.

For the short-term future, there is likely to be much trauma associated with work for a variety of reasons stated previously. In the longer range future, work may become more satisfying and a less important part of our lives.

Less Time for Leisure Among Those in the Labor Force

There is little doubt that the proportion of our lives spent at work has decreased greatly during this century. Owen (1969) found that the proportion of life spent in work time for U.S. males decreased from 23 percent in 1900 to 15 percent in 1960. A primary cause for this was the increasing proportion of one's life spent out of the labor force as well as reductions in workweek length. Declines in workweek length ceased to be dramatic in the late 1940s and any further reduction in work time came primarily from earlier retirement in relation to life expectancy and more paid holidays and vacations.

There are a number of indications, however, that during the last decade the amount of leisure available has declined, at least for those who are not retired. First we have the largest percentage of our population in the labor force we have ever had. Overall, employment grew 16 percent from 1979 to 1985 (U.S. Bureau of Labor Statistics, 1987). This is due primarily to the huge increase in women working outside the home but also to a higher percentage of working teenagers. A Louis Harris survey (1987) reported a decline in time for leisure among adults from 26.2 hours per week in 1973 to only 16.6 hours per week in 1987. (See Figure 3). This drop was associated partly with an increase in hours worked, from 40.6 to 47.3, due to the shift toward a service economy and more salaried workers, who generally work longer hours. It was also associated with an increase in time spent commuting, going to school, studying and keeping house as more adults go back to school and women combine family, housework and job responsibilities. Men, according to Harris, had an average of 20.3 hours for leisure each week while women had only 15.6.

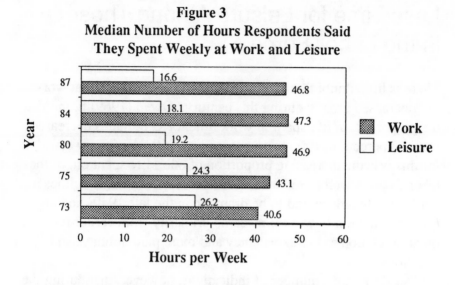

Figure 3
Median Number of Hours Respondents Said
They Spent Weekly at Work and Leisure

Cited in *New York Times,* March 16, 1988, p.24.

Those with higher income now work longer hours than those with lesser ones. (One wonders what Karl Marx or Thorstein Veblen would have made of this.) Additionally, Harris found that those with long hours included small-business people, mainly retailers, who worked an average of 57.3 hours a week with only 14.3 hours left for leisure; professional people who worked 52.2 hours per week with only 16.9 hours of leisure; those with incomes over $50,000 per year who worked 52.4 hours per week with 16.9 hours a week for leisure; members of the Baby Boom Generation who worked 51.9 hours per week with 15.7 hours of leisure available; Yuppies, who worked 52.7 hours per week with only 17.1 hours left for leisure; women, who worked 48.9 hours per week and had 16.4 hours of leisure per week; and college graduates who worked 52.9 hours a week and had 18.0 hours of leisure (Harris, 1987). After surveying these changes, Harris (1987) drew the following conclusions:

More people are now considering more carefully what to commit their leisure time to, including how

to get uninterrupted rest. This means that decisions
on time commitment are being made not in terms
of the cost of leisure activities but on the basis of
the most desirable way to spend scarce hours. In
the future, if people want to spend time in something
badly enough, they are likely to find the money to
do it. Up to now, the assumption has been that if
people have the money to do something and want
to commit to it, they would find the time
(Harris, 1987).

More Flexible Work Arrangements

While industrialization produced highly regimented, centralized work arrangements in factories, changes in the kinds of work done, in the composition of households and in technological advances have all led to work becoming more flexible, even if it is more pervasive. As Naisbett (1982) noted, we have gone from an economy which involved most workers in the production of goods to one which involved them in the production of services to one which involves them in the production of information. Two- and three-worker families have also necessitated changes in working schedules designed to accommodate one-worker families. Microcomputers and other technological advances have made it possible to work at home or produce almost any product from almost any location.

In regard to working schedules, the percentage of people working fulltime but less than five days a week is growing four times faster than the rest of the labor force (Noble, 1988). Those working at least 40 hours a week in more than five-day week schedules have grown by eight percent. Over 12 percent of all workers now have schedules which allow them to vary their starting and finishing times. An increasing number of companies use "floating holidays" which allow employees to use one or more days as needed throughout the year. In spite of such changes, the majority of workers continue to work a five-day, 40 hour week.

The Unknown Impact of Sudden Technological Advance

In numerous areas of life, our society may be rapidly changed by a variety of technological advances. While no systematic treatment can be given here of such advances, some examples may suffice. In presenting these examples, it is not assumed that the potential for technological advance will automatically mean such changes take place. Some, such as the ability to produce a car which emits almost no air pollution, have already been suppressed by auto manufacturers for several years since it would mean monumental retooling costs. Other technological changes may be increasingly judged by society as dangerous and, therefore, outlawed. Perhaps one example of this is the technique of oxygenating the brain prior to birth to enhance intelligence. Another example is the development of a "sober-up" pill or an abortion pill, both of which are technically feasible in the short-term future. What would the social consequences be of sobering up with a single pill anyone who has consumed alcohol? Would it prevent accidents, encourage underage drinking, lead to an increase in alcohol consumption? Similarly, how would an abortion pill affect the sexual behavior and values of people? The answers to such questions are unknown.

The potential for technological breakthroughs to revolutionize behavior is expanding exponentially. The prospect of superconductivity of electricity could lead to massive reduction in costs and eliminate any nuclear generation. Would such a breakthrough lead to a higher standard of living? Would it encourage yet more consumption of other goods which require electricity and therefore actually speed up the depletion of scarce resources within the world? No one can say. A universal translating machine, possibly looking like a "Walkman" with a microphone for speaking as well as earphones, has the potential to revolutionize foreign travel, relations among diplomats, business people, the French and English speaking peoples of Canada, the citizens of the soon-to-be united Europe, and others. Moreover, the impact of such a device would have far-reaching consequences on freedom of speech, spying, and popular culture. The decisions made in designing the software for such a machine could change whole cultural traditions.

It is in the area of medicine and health that mere technological capacity increasingly will not be sufficient to justify some medical procedure. The potential for multiple organ transplants, the ability to create chimeras (part animal and part human), the development of artificial blood (which is almost a reality at this writing), the extensive use of bionics to replace virtually every human part, chemical methods of memory enhancement, hibernational techniques, artificial knowledge transfer, the potential for participatory evolution in which offspring are increasing designed by the parents or the state will all create the need to make decisions about our preferred futures. Such decisions will be necessary because the cost of such technology will be, initially, monumental and will prevent the expenditure of funds in other needed health-related areas such as educational approaches aimed at minimizing health risks. We will also have to decide how much future shock we can stand, how much we think the world needs improving and what level of risks we will take to bring about such changes.

The Coming War Over Human Consciousness

All of the problems of the environment discussed in the last section may be attributed to a larger problem — faulty human perception. According to such a viewpoint, problems of pollution, the misuse of resources, even human health are all part of an inability to accurately perceive the world. Our consciousness, in other words, is false. It has been argued (for example, Rifkin, 1987; Grof, 1988; Capra, 1988) that two modes of human consciousness exist. One mode, which Grof refers to as Cartesian-Newtonian, perceives reality as separate objects existing in three-dimensional space. Time, in this concept, exists as a straight line. Such a line of reasoning, others have argued, stresses the rational nature of humans who are thought to be able to use logic and technique to reform nature to meet their own ends. According to Grof (1988):

> A person functioning exclusively in the Cartesian mode may be free from manifest symptoms but cannot be considered mentally healthy. Such individuals typically lead ego-centered, competitive, goal-oriented lives. They tend to be unable to derive satisfaction from ordinary activities in everyday life and become alienated from their inner world. For people whose existence is dominated by this mode of experience no level of wealth, power or fame will bring satisfaction. They become infused with a sense of meaninglessness, futility and even absurdity that no amount of external success can dispel.

A second way of viewing the world may be called, variously, spiritual, holistic, or transpersonal. According to such perceptual bases, reality must be viewed as a series of relationships among all things which are part of some universal consciousness. Humans are part of this universal system, and neither humans nor the larger system which they are a part of are completely knowable through science.

This fundamental division in perception increasingly shapes different visions of the world and of what future is to be desired. Architects may design buildings which they view as fortresses or as structures which blend harmoniously with nature. Psychiatrists may view mental illness as an individual who has gone "crazy" or as an organism making an appropriate response to a crazy situation or, indeed, a crazy world. Agriculture may view nature as simply a resource which can be exploited with chemicals, machines and technique in a battle for more food; or nature may be viewed as a complex series of interrelationships which must be minimally changed in growing food.

Such a division has even brought about increasingly different conceptualizations of time. As Rifkin (1987) pointed out, these two fundamentally different concepts of time lead to different politically viewpoints and prescriptions concerning the future:

> The new time spectrum runs from empathetic
> rhythms on one side to power rhythms on the other.
> Those who align themselves with the empathetic
> time dynamic are calling for the "resacralization"
> of life at every level of existence from microbe to
> man. Those aligning themselves with the power
> time dynamic are calling for a more efficient simu-
> lated environment to secure the general well-being
> of society. The rhythm of the first constituency is
> slow-paced, rhapsodic, spontaneous, vulnerable and
> participatory. Emphasis is upon reestablishing a
> temporal communion with the natural biological
> and physical rhythms and of coexisting in harmony
> with the cycles, seasons and periodicities of the
> larger earth organism. The rhythms of the other
> side are accelerated, predictable and expedient.
> Emphasis is upon subsuming the natural biological

and physical rhythms and creating an artificially
controlled environment that can assure an ever-
increasing growth curve for present and future
generations (Rifkin, 1987).

Thus, one perception seeks to speed up the world and to
remove time from the definitions of nature to bring about perpetual
material growth while another wants to reintegrate our notion of
time with nature, place limits on our desire, and accept that we
have no capacity for perfectibility outside of nature.

Certainly the former concept has led to some fundamental
changes in our use of time and our leisure behavior.

SECTION TWO—
THRIVING ON CHANGE

What do the previous changes mean to the leisure service profession? If they mean one single thing, they mean we are going to change, although part of such change may be remembering some of our old beliefs. Because the important arena for action has become the local and the global, the generalizations made here will have to be altered to fit unique local situations. We have no effective way to act globally yet, other than by individual example at the local level. Such individual example is a critical part, but only a part, of the complex equation which will determine whether we survive and prosper. It will also change our definition of what "prospering" means.

In responding to the changes discussed, recreation, park and leisure service professionals will be challenged, first and foremost, to be actors rather than reactors in the change process. We must avoid the mistake of the railroad executives who believed, until it was too late, that they were in the railroad business when what they were really in was the transportation business. There are a number of different organizational alternatives for the provision of leisure services. They must be experimented with. There are many good reasons to change relationships within such organizations among various staff. Such reasons must be acted upon. There is lots of evidence that the area of life we traditionally deal with has changed in meaning and content. Such changes must be recognized in both conceptual and operational terms. The lines between public and private are harder to draw. The vagueness of such boundaries must be accepted.

The following is more the basis for thoughtfulness about responding to change in leisure service delivery than it is a prescription. Some of what follows has been influenced by the writings of management expert Tom Peters, although his work has dealt primarily with the private sector.

The Coming Reform

There is every indication that we will enter an era of profound reform during the next decade. Such reform is urgently needed because our ways of life are currently, to put it simply, inappropriate. Socially inappropriate because we have not yet adjusted to the new kinds and styles of primary social groups which have emerged. This has made many of us more vulnerable, less educated and less socialized into our former ways of life. Economically inappropriate because we continue to make false assumptions about our personal and collective financial capabilities. Additionally, we are failing to provide for those who are financially impoverished, even though the evidence is overwhelming that we can do so. Ecologically inappropriate because we are doing major harm to air, water, vegetation, and forms of animal life which are necessary to sustain our survival and essential parts of the single whole which is the earth.

These inappropriate ways of living stem from false perception. Our perception is that we can continue to have unlimited economic growth, unlimited leisure experience, unlimited life. Our perception is, often, that we are distinct entities whose fate is not related to the fate of others. To a great extent, these beliefs were fueled by our unprecedented economic situation which resulted from unique conditions at the end of the second world war.

To a great extent, also, our society is today merely recreating a cycle of unbridled individual and organizational greed leading to the need for societal control which has taken place at various times throughout history. During medieval times, for example, common land owned by everyone was carefully regulated to control its productivity. As these controls broke down, however, farmers found themselves in the situation of having an incentive to graze as many animals as they could since, if they didn't, someone else would. The result was overgrazing, which ruined the commons for everyone (Hardin, 1978). When such controls or regulations break down, the individual is in a double bind, either restraining him or herself and feeling like a fool or exploiting the situation and feeling guilty. Hardin suggested that the solution to such situations is "mutual coercion mutually agreed upon" (Hardin, 1968). Society must agree to coerce those who act irresponsibly. Such coercion can already be seen in our own society in the formation of neighborhood crime watches and joint action against local drug dealers. In many cases, however, government will have to be involved. How does a neighborhood, for example, take action against a corporation which has dumped poisonous chemicals in landfills around the country without the action amounting to vigilantism?

The coming reform era will give leisure service professionals a renewed opportunity to do what they have historically done best — help other people. The parks and recreation movement was born and nurtured in a spirit of reform. It is what we know best. Public leisure services (and, in some cases, private ones) are not at home in the marketing model; they are more appropriately belief driven. While marketing public leisure services makes sense in a nearly perfect world, since, in such a world, people have had exposure to a broad range of leisure experiences and sufficient education, health and income to enable them to identify what is "good" for them, in our society such conditions do not exist for considerable segments of the population. The child raised by the television wants more television, the ghetto teenager who knows only the basketball court wants more basketball. The adult who has never had poetry read to him or her is unlikely to desire poetry. The leisure service professional, therefore, must start not only with the question: "What do people want?" but also with the questions: "What does the world need?" and "What can people learn to want?"

The Central Issue of Quality

So much has been said about quality during the last few years that we have a tendency to become numb to what it means. Nevertheless, for leisure service organizations to prosper during the next decade, the quality of service will have to be increased tremendously in virtually every facet of their operations. Let's review the reasons for this. First and foremost, Americans believe that recreation and leisure are a part of their lives which is of critical importance. They will respond positively to an agency's services only if employees' actions show them that they also think it is of central importance. Ironically, thinking that recreation and leisure are important may be negatively related to supporting public recreation and park agencies, which may sometimes be viewed as providing trivial, irrelevant or second-rate services. As our society ages, customers of leisure services will become more critical, since older people tend to be more judgmental. Also, because we are in a period of increasing economic restraint, people are cutting back their recreation and leisure activities and are much more demanding about the activities which remain. The amount of leisure which working people have has decreased over the past few years and the leisure which remains has become more highly planned and specialized. As education levels have increased, people have been exposed to a wider range of leisure behaviors and have developed higher expectations about the benefits of leisure experience. People with higher levels of education also have higher levels of expectation about the environmental and aesthetic aspects of their leisure experience. For all these reasons and many more, the services provided by recreation, park and leisure service organizations will have to make quantum leaps in quality to be viable.

How does one begin to increase quality? For the leisure service professional, it must begin with the realization that leisure, rather than being a small part of life which is used merely to get ready to work again, has become the central arena for self-expression in our culture, as it already has in many others. The public knows this, but many in the recreation, park and leisure profession don't. Perhaps they don't because they have been in a comparatively low status occupation which has been concerned, like those in the lower-middle class, with respectability. Do your job, don't take risks, don't make waves, don't attract attention to yourself, and convince yourself that the public doesn't understand. Perhaps the public does understand; we don't.

While the public does understand, it may be using different words than we are accustomed to. "Quality of life" is a concept that the public understands and values. That term includes, or should include, public recreation, park and leisure services. Quality of life means that every square foot of park land counts. It means every person in the community, every tree, every foot of sidewalk, every fast food restaurant, every crime, every editorial in the newspaper, every softball game matters. It matters if there is graffiti in the park, it matters if the snack bar in the zoo has an appropriate, interesting menu. It matters if someone responds immediately to a citizen who walks into a municipal recreation and park department office seeking to find out what's going on. It matters, and it is going to matter more and more. Recreation, park and leisure services are the backbone organization in shaping the quality of life in most communities, but employees of such agencies generally don't realize it.

We are so used to being considered secondary in importance that it is hard to realize that our importance is now primary. What this means, however, is that we must remember our dream; put it back into our head. We must demand the best, from those who work for us, from those we serve and from ourselves.

Rethinking the Organization of Leisure Services

We are in not only a period of rapid societal change but also a management revolution. It is increasingly recognized that top-down management with several layers of bureaucracy makes no sense. In a period of change in which many of the changes are unpredictable, leisure service organizations must develop increased flexibility and rethink every facet of the organization. Doing this will mean reconceptualizing many functions of a leisure service agency. Let's take, as an example, maintenance.

Currently, maintenance is often a low status and isolated function of public recreation, park and leisure service agencies. Employees are often comparatively low paid and receive little on-the-job training. In many instances, they are not involved in planning, programming, budgeting, or evaluating within the department. This situation is a disaster and changing it is critical to the success of leisure service agencies of the future.

Perhaps the first thing to do in changing this situation is to recognize what "maintenance" must become for leisure service agencies to survive — Environmental Quality Control. Environmental quality control is the most important task of a leisure service agency. It is most important because our population is getting older, and older people are much more sensitive to aesthetics of their environment, cleanliness, natural beauty, safety and other quality control issues. It is important because it helps teach the young that one's immediate environment is of great consequence and, therefore, so are the individuals in it. It is most important because our society is acquiring more formal education and individuals with more formal education have higher expectations concerning quality of environment; particularly leisure environments. The condition and qualities of the leisure environment are often a critical factor in their decision to use or not use a given leisure area or facility. Certainly Walt Disney has known this for

years; certainly McDonald's understands this. Certainly the
managers of many resorts and hotels understand this. As leisure
experience has become more central to the lives of millions of
Americans, a given act of participation is viewed as a total experience rather than participation in a given activity. Increasingly,
leisure will consist of being with friends voluntarily in a pleasing
environment. If the environment isn't pleasing, people will go
elsewhere.

Maintenance will also be thought of in the future as being
directly related to the law enforcement function. The level of
maintenance, cleanliness of the area and state of repair provide
"cues" to users as to what is acceptable behavior; whether or not
the park or recreation area in question really matters. Since
children and adolescents tend to be imitative, the cues they receive
from the maintenance conditions in the park may help determine
whether they decide to commit an act of vandalism, litter or
otherwise deface the site. Thus, environmental quality control and
crime prevention are related.

Maintenance workers are not only involved in environmental quality control; they are also involved directly in leisure
programming. Such employees ultimately help determine where
and upon what people sit when they have a picnic in a public park,
what they see when they are eating their meal, whether visiting a
restroom will break the mood of celebration, whether or not their
mood is shaped by bright or soft colors on public buildings,
whether or not they feel they have entered an environment which
those in charge feel is important, how far and on what they walk to
a tennis court, swimming pool or softball field, and many other
decisions which directly shape or "program" the behavior of those
who visit a leisure environment. Maintenance, or environmental
quality control, is the single most tangible and immediate indicator
of quality to the visitor, participant or customer.

Many maintenance workers are often isolated from the
agency for which they work, undertrained, underappreciated,
devoid of understanding of what their organization in question
wishes to accomplish, and left out of most or all agency planning.

In effect, maintenance workers are expected, in many instances, simply to deal with what has been planned and programmed as best they can in complete isolation from the process which produced the planning and programming. This won't do. Maintenance workers will have to understand and be involved in each and every aspect of their agency's undertakings.

Managers of specific parks, particularly state and country parks, also will have to change. First, there must be the recognition that, while national, state, county or municipal parks may be part of a system, the uniqueness of each park— in terms of visitors, landscape, aesthetics, history, behavior patterns of visitors and otherwise— far outweighs any similarities the park has with other parks. In an era of regionalization and decentralization, the process of developing and administering parks must be, as park historian Galen Cranz (1982) stated, a process of "cultural discovery" rather than one of technology. That means you must start from scratch with each park, start from scratch each budget year, start from scratch each day. Most parks are used by a specific subset of the population which lives in relatively close proximity to the park. This is also true for other public and private facilities such as libraries and restaurants. Because parks are generally used by an identifiable subset of the population, and because these users will have increasingly higher expectations about these parks at the very time that government, because of overspending, is pushing recreation, park and leisure services to generate income, the park manager will have to change roles quickly and drastically. These new roles will be as host and as community organizer.

The park manager must become a host for a variety of reasons. First, as LaPage (1983) and others have noted, people who visit parks want questions answered, want contact with those who are responsible for the park, want the assurance that someone is in charge. Older people feel comforted when the manager is visible and responsive to their needs. As the public become increasingly critical leisure consumers, the park manager must be proactive, out front, talking with his or her "customers" who have chosen that leisure environment over others. This means getting out of the office and also getting park "customers" into his or her office. This means seeking input from visitors, insisting that ways be found to obtain input from park customers and, where appropriate, acting immediately upon their concerns. This process of obtaining input means that the park host must involve other park staff in this process on a continuous, rather than one shot, basis. It may mean that environmental quality control staff need to sit down in the park host's office with a group of picnickers who have just spent some time in the park to get their comments on how the picnic went and how it could have been improved. It may mean a suggestion box in the park with prizes given for the best suggestion. It will definitely mean a system by which park staff can make specific suggestions for change and be rewarded for making these suggestions. Most important, of course, it means acting on these suggestions, even if doing so disrupts the routine of work. Ultimately, this process will have to become routine.

Certainly, it may be argued that many state and federal parks are currently full to overflowing and the above is therefore not necessary. For the park manager, the criterion of success in the past — attendance — will no longer be the criterion of success in the future. A full park may or may not indicate a successful park just as a full school or hospital may not indicate that they are successful. What happens to the visitor and to the environment in which the visit takes place will be critical to definitions of success or failure.

Park law enforcement may undergo drastic changes in the next few decades, starting with a reconceptualization of what tasks are entailed. Park police, like police elsewhere, are likely to become "guides," except for a few highly trained personnel among them who will continue to serve a more traditional police function. Part of the reason for this change will be in the increasing recognition that it is more cost effective to try to take a "prevention" approach to crime than to deal with those who have committed crime. As reported elsewhere in this book, only about one reported crime in five leads to an arrest. Since much crime is not reported and a huge proportion of arrests don't lead to conviction, our present system has a high probability of failure. Furthermore, the traditional police function has always been modified, to some extent, within park environments due not only to the nature of the park environment but also to the nature of crimes which are likely to be committed in parks. This modification of the law enforcement and crime prevention function is likely to become more pronounced, with "park police" associating more with park work than police work. Park police in the future, while they will continue to use what B. F. Skinner (1978) called "aversive conditioning" (punishment for undesired acts), will put more emphasis upon "nonaversive conditioning" (rewarding people for changing undesirable behavior). They will also increasingly use positive reinforcement (rewarding people for desirable behavior). In many ways, this will make the park law enforcement job a more pleasant one, since the park law enforcement staff will be in the position of rewarding individuals as well as punishing them. Park guides (police) will seek to be non-threatening in appearance, knowledgeable about the park and all facets of its operation, will initiate contacts with individuals and groups using the park, perhaps asking if they can be of help in any way, and will otherwise seek to assist the visitor. Already there are some park systems in which park police issue "positive" citations for exemplary behavior among park users, sometimes accompanied by a small gift or fee waiver for a future visit. Such an approach reinforces positive behavior and provides a model for other park users to follow.

All this, of course, means that park police will have to be highly familiar with the park and all aspects of its operations. For this to happen, they will need to be more highly integrated into the organization of the recreation and park or park department in question, attending department meetings, making input on planning decisions and otherwise functioning as part of the park agency rather than a paramilitary organization. Like maintenance staff, park planners and others, park police will have to be less isolated from the day-to-day operations of the park department and its staff. Park police will also undertake more of their traditional task of law enforcement more indirectly, encouraging and educating park users in methods of self-policing. These efforts may take a number of forms, from encouraging and organizing volunteer "park watch" patrols to the use of various types of audio-visual materials to talking with park users and special interest recreation groups about how they can help minimize crime in the parks.

The previous is not meant to indicate that park police will abandon their traditional law enforcement role. Such a role, however, will be fulfilled by a much smaller number of highly trained specialists, who will undertake detective work and make arrests where necessary. Such specialists will not be involved in routine "patrol" of recreation and park properties. Patrol will become visitation with park users, serving a hospitality function, an information function and a crime prevention and detection function. Those involved in this function will be in contact with the law enforcement specialists through a number of increasingly sophisticated electronic means and may use video tape to document evidence thought to be related to crime.

Like many other recreation and park functions, law enforcement will, in the future, stress prevention of crime and education of park users concerning the consequences of crime, will incorporate a teaching and hospitality function into their duties, will be more highly integrated into their parent agency, and will encourage the public to take a larger role in the function of crime prevention.

If maintenance, management and law enforcement will change, the position of "recreation programmer," as currently conceived, will largely disappear. First, the idea of "program," which has meant structured leisure activities, will have to be vastly broadened since, as previously discussed, the leisure environment is a critical part of the individual participant's experience and recreation programmers have often been only minimally involved with the environmental aspects of leisure experience. Second, the idea that there is a "basic" or "standard" program makes virtually no sense. How people use leisure and how a given leisure service agency can facilitate that process will have to be defined through investigation in each situation and then continuously redefined though constant contact with the clientele or potential clientele or customers of the agency in question. The "recreation programmer" will become a "leisure scientist" and a "leisure catalyst." While all members of a leisure service agency will be involved in some way with every aspect of the leisure experiences of those they serve, the former recreation programmer will be more specialized in understanding leisure behavior. This understanding will be based not only upon academic coursework dealing with leisure from philosophical, sociological and psychological aspects, but also upon the ability to conduct and interpret research concerning many aspects of recreation and leisure for the clientele. Much of this research will likely be "qualitative," that is, it will not consist of huge surveys and complex statistics but instead will use "ethnomethodology," a big word meaning mainly that the researcher will try to understand things from the perception of those being studied, rather than from the assumptions about that group which the researcher makes in advance. As recreation and leisure have become more important and less standardized in our culture, the former "recreation programmer" will become a "leisure scientist," interested not in generalizations which can be made about leisure behavior for the entire population nor in the discovery of eternal scientific truths about leisure, but rather in the constantly changing daily lives of those served by the agency in question and how these conditions should shape the services offered.

The "recreation programmer" will also be a "leisure catalyst," making things happen in the community or among the clients or customers in question as a result of knowledge obtained through ongoing practical research and consultation. This catalytic process will be continuous and will constitute a perpetual experiment. While many former concepts of recreation professionals implied that they should serve an "enabler" or "facilitator" role, in the next decade the emphasis will be upon the research prior to facilitation. The recreation program will be of less concern than the leisure environment and the information needs in order to facilitate a leisure environment will increase exponentially. The leisure catalyst role will be one in which information gained from research is widely shared with a variety of groups in order to generate ideas and visions which lead to changes in services delivered. The groups to whom research is communicated and how it is communicated will vary greatly. The leisure catalyst role will involve working with business people, homeowners' associations, homeless people, teenagers, state departments of transportation, drug rehabilitation centers, universities, tavern owners, lesbian and gay organizations, etc. The "leisure scientist-catalyst" will need a car but may not need an office.

Therapeutic recreation professionals are already in a process of changing what they do and why. This change will result in them becoming "leisure educators" with two thrusts: developing appropriate leisure behaviors and independent leisure behaviors. These roles will be undertaken with a broader clientele, which has in common a wide range of conditions and situations which make them more highly dependent on others to facilitate their leisure expression and/or current involvement in leisure behaviors which are defined by society as inappropriate. If educating for independent and appropriate leisure expression is the evolving goal, the evolving means of reaching that goal is likely to be educating those who work with various groups who are highly leisure dependent or who use leisure inappropriately. In an informal way, this means educating those who are potential educators rather than working directly with individuals in such groups. This will mean that the leisure educator (therapeutic recreation specialist) will train/educate those who work in nursing homes, those who work with the physically handicapped, the addicted, those in the culture of poverty, those who are "institutionalized" or incarcerated, those who have suffered traumatic life events such as the death of a spouse, those in the armed forces, those whose parents have divorced, and many other groups.

Leisure educators will work with their clients indirectly rather than directly for a number of reasons, some of them financial. If we take the provision of recreation and leisure to those in nursing homes, for example, we see the problem. As the number of individuals in nursing homes increases dramatically it will be increasing expensive to hire qualified full-time employees to provide direct leisure services for residents. Rather, leisure educators will train those who work in nursing homes or serve as volunteers.

Tom Peters (1987) described companies of the 1990s which will succeed as having the following characteristics: (1) flatter — fewer layers of organization, (2) populated by more autonomous units, (3) oriented toward differentiation, producing high value-added goods and services, (4) quality conscious, (5) service conscious, (6) more responsive, (7) much faster at innovation, (8) a user of highly trained, flexible people as the principal means of adding value. All leisure service employees will need to change if leisure service organizations are to be re-shaped in the previous ways.

Planning for Life Cycles

Much of the trouble our country is in is due to planning for the
short-term future, planning for immediate profit, planning for the
creation of something but not for its continuance, growth, gradual
decline and ultimate death. Our corporations, unlike the Japanese,
look for short-term gain rather than long-term stability, incre-
mental growth and improvement. Much of what we call planning
has actually dealt with only the birth of some service, facility or
product. The various entities involved in planning a shopping
center, for instance, often plan only for the "development" of the
physical structure — drainage, sewerage, access roads, the design
and location of buildings, etc. Shopping malls tend to look quite
different after 25 years but "planners" rarely consider the life cycle
of the mall. The corporation which owns it usually seeks only to
rent space within the mall for as long as it is profitable and then get
out. Some second home development planning extends only to the
point at which all properties are sold and the governance is turned
over to an owners' association. Municipal governments plan
where they will store their garbage during the next decade but,
often, not longer. Examples abound of the extent to which our
planning is short-term and fails to think of what is planned in terms
of its life cycle. Perhaps part of the reason for this has been the
arrogance which our privileged position in the world gave us. We
didn't have to plan long term, we thought, because we had the
resources to fix whatever went wrong. We also believed that
science and technology could cure any problems which emerged.
Planning has been frankly suspect in our culture in many quarters
because we equated much of it with limits on our freedom, creep-
ing socialism, and an insult to our rugged individualism. There has
also been the argument that business, if left alone by planners,
would naturally and automatically do what is best and right for the
American people.

Our situation today is such that planning for the long term
is simply necessary. Our society is more interdependent, more

vulnerable, and more subject to a variety of potential ecological disasters. There is also less ability to "throw money" at problems caused or made worse by short-term or no planning. Planning will have to be longer term and holistic. That is, to realize that everything done in the world ultimately affects the whole world since we are all, as are dogs, airplanes and the Mississippi River, part of the same thing.

In recreation and parks, some of the planning in the past has not been able to incorporate this approach. The Land and Water Conservation Fund, for instance, while it has done enormous good, did not take a holistic planning approach. The federal government made moneys available to "plan, acquire and develop" outdoor recreation areas and facilities. Once this process took place, however, the mission was viewed as complete by administrators of the fund. The planning consequences of the fund, however, continue today. Since the fund created many new outdoor recreation areas and facilities for local governments, these added greatly to the maintenance costs of local government on a continuing basis. Local government could therefore generate more revenue, perhaps through taxes or fees for use of new outdoor recreation areas and facilities, undertake less maintenance per unit on their areas and facilities, or, hopefully, become more efficient in terms of maintenance. Because the fund required some local and state financial contribution, wealthier communities benefitted disproportionately, thus increasing the gap between rich and poor (Burdick, 1978). Thus, in very tangible ways, failure to plan for the long-term future had unanticipated consequences. Rather than providing for the planning, acquisition and development of, say, a swimming pool, ways must be found to plan for the pool's life cycle. Such planning will bring leisure service professionals in more direct contact with all other forms of planning and with a diversity of types of information. Leisure services planning will become, increasingly, long-term, concerned with maximum flexibility or multiple options and integrated into the rest of the planning effort, both public and private, which takes place within their region. It is not farfetched to say that many large-scale leisure services will be planned using the world as the basic planning unit.

Increased Specialization in Leisure Behavior

There are a number of indications that people in our society will increasingly "specialize" in some forms of leisure behavior during the next decade. Bryan referred to recreation specialization as "as a continuum of behavior from the general to the particular, reflected by equipment and skills used in the sport and activity setting preferences" (Bryan, 1979). As one becomes more specialized in a leisure behavior he or she goes from being a beginner who has few expectations about the activity and simply wants to get some kind of result to a second stage where the activity becomes an established behavior and the participant wants to validate competence through a number of successes or greater challenges. At the third level, according to Bryan, the participant becomes highly specialized in a number of aspects of participation, such as equipment. Many specialists get interested in some specific mode of participation or aspect of it. Someone interested in hunting may specialize in quail hunting. A stamp collector may become interested only in buying and selling rare stamps. At this level of specialization in a leisure activity, the participant wants to participate with others who are similarly specialized. At the fourth level of specialization, the participant places "the most emphasis on doing the activity for its own sake" (Bryan, 1979). Such individuals place the most emphasis upon the "quality" of the experience and make the most demands on the leisure resource setting. For the specialist in a leisure experience, quality of experience is all-important.

There is every indication that, while many forms of leisure expression today are done for recovery from work and the frantic pace of life, there is a growing trend toward specialization. Increased specialized in leisure behaviors is occurring for many reasons. An older population with more formal education and more exposure to leisure experiences has led to increased specialization. As Yankelovich, Skelly and White (1986) reported, a weakening of the "experience thrust" of the 1970s, due to tougher times economically and a recognition of the social problems it produced, "encouraged many consumers — less concerned about novelty or maximizing experience — to narrow their repertoire of interests. Consequently, many leisure activities . . . have begun to consolidate around a core market of individuals committed to developing advanced skills in a particular field of interest" (Yankelovich, Skelly and White, 1986).

What does the increasing phenomenon of specialization mean to recreation, park and leisure service professionals? It may mean, one is tempted to say, that those in leisure services should cut back as much as they can on what they provide and provide the very highest quality of service with what remains. It certainly means that a given activity label, such as "sailing," no longer conveys how the experience should be managed. Managers of leisure environments must understand the level of specialization of those who are likely to participate and what qualitative aspects are appropriate. Increased specialization in leisure behavior may mean that the participant will be willing to pay more for quality but will not participate when such quality is absent.

The trends toward specialization in leisure behavior will make leisure service professionals recognize anew what Marshall McLuhan told us in 1964: "The medium is the message" (McLuhan, 1964). Leisure environments are, in effect, media within which people have leisure experiences and these environments, to a great extent, define the leisure experience. The leisure medium within which behavior takes place is, in effect, the leisure message which the participant receives. The conditions, aesthetics, location, level of maintenance, and other characteristics of the park define what the picnic means. "Picnic" doesn't mean much until it is placed within a given leisure environment or medium. Then the leisure medium defines the leisure message to the participant. As McLuhan observed: "What we are considering here . . . are the psychic and social consequences of the designs or patterns as they amplify or accelerate existing processes. For the 'message' of any medium or technology is the change of scale or pace or pattern that it introduces into human affairs" (McLuhan, 1964). What are the psychic and social consequences of a given tennis environment on the pattern of behavior which takes place in that environment and on the "message" in the mind of the tennis player? For the increasingly specialized leisure participant, the "medium" in which a leisure experience occurs will increasingly be the "message" of the quality of experience. There is, in effect, no generic "medium" of a tennis environment. Each tennis environment is a different medium which produces a different message. If the message is not positive, the participant will seek a different medium. For the non-specialized participant in a leisure behavior, almost any message will do, so almost any environment will do. As the participant becomes more specialized, the medium is the message.

The specialization of participation in many forms of leisure expression represents the reversal of a trend of increased mass production and "commodification" of leisure experience which occurred over the last few decades. Butsch (1984) provided us with an example of this with his intensive study of the model airplane hobby and industry. He found that three periods were evident in model airplane building: a first phase in which there were no commercial kits for making planes, a second phase in which hobbyists lost control of the "means of production" to companies, whose owners stayed in close contact with their hobby customers, and a third stage in which "the hobby itself is shaped by the demands of a capitalist industry" (Butsch, 1984). This process of increasing standardization of a leisure behavior to meet the needs of a corporation is being reversed today not only because of a recognition on the part of a more educated public that this system was increasingly devoid of meaning, but also because increased entrepreneurship has resulted in a wide variety of ways to learn about and participate in the activity.

The advent of increased specialization in leisure activities will mean that the amount of knowledge about specific forms of leisure behavior will have to increase for those in the planning process. More important, it will mean that planning of such leisure environments will have to be done with the continued, direct, in the office, in-your-face participation of those who are specialists in the leisure behavior in question. Design of leisure environments, in effect, will have to be done much more specifically for those who will use that particular environment. This follows not only from trends in specialized leisure behavior but also from consumer expectations for customized, specialized products.

Retrofitting for an Aging Society

As our society rapidly ages, leisure services will have to be retrofitted to meet rapidly changing needs. In doing this, it is likely that renewed attention will be given, at the same time, to children and youth. In one sense, these changes will be part of the increasing customization of services and products going on in many facets of our society. Changing leisure services in ways which make them more relevant to older people will require imagination and experimentation. The current generation of elderly does not provide a very good model for future generations of older citizens since the now-elderly have lower levels of health and formal education than will the coming generation. Additionally, the coming generations of older Americans will have a broader repertoire of leisure activities, fewer differences between the genders in terms of use of leisure and will place higher importance upon recreation and leisure expression.

Rather than planning for the "elderly" or, worse yet, "senior citizens," it will make more sense to plan inclusively for later life. There is considerable evidence that those in later life agree on a number of issues concerning the provision of leisure services, such as the central important of safety, maintenance, the natural environment, socialization and appropriate food and drink. This is not to imply that people get more alike as they age; in many ways they become more diverse. It does appear, however, that many leisure environments will have to be radically altered to be made more useful for an aging public. Let us take the example of a swimming pool, such as might be found at a private swimming club. Many of such pools seem to have been designed for the tiny fraction of the population, mostly young, who go to a swimming pool and mainly swim. Most people who are visiting a swim club or public swimming pool are not in the water for the majority of time they are there. Of those who are in the water, the majority are not swimming. The design of the pool is often highly inappropriate for older people who want to be able to descend into the water slowly rather than dive in, want to be able to sit down while in the water and talk with friends, want shade in close proximity to the pool, want snacks which are not full of salt and sugar, want to avoid heavy metal rock music from either boom boxes or a loud speaker above the snack bar, want evidence of the natural environment and tasteful decor and clean restrooms. In short, they want a swimming pool that is appropriate.

Providing leisure services for and with those in later life will also mean that more attention must be given to many forms of voluntary learning which a more highly educated population will seek out. If we exclude vocational adult education, it may be said that in the near future the line between what is adult education service and what is leisure service will almost disappear. Pleasurable learning has a healthy future, and formats and styles must now be found to make such opportunities appropriate and available. Adult learning would seem particularly appropriate as a use of leisure in the near future. It does not consume huge amounts of material goods, can be relatively low cost to the participant, can allow for differing degrees of specialization on the part of the learner, from dabbler to scholar, has little negative impact on the environment, has the potential to be of central importance in the life of an older person, may develop skills in the learner which help him or her cope with society's problems, and helps foster both personal independence and, often, a sense of community from interacting with other adult learners.

Recreation and park professionals and adult educators will be working directly with each other. In fact, in an era in which narrow occupational specialties within the professions are going to be de-emphasized, recreation and park and adult education professionals may become each other.

Responding to the Needs of Children

Historically, recreation services in the public sector as well as some park services came into being out of direct concern for the plight of poor children in urban areas. The process of urbanization took place due to the extensive development of industry. Almost no social planning took place. Consequently, many children and adolescents were left without any place to play and, often, without many of their developmental needs attended to. The settlement house movement, the play movement, the character development initiatives all tried to address the needs of youth. One of the most import assumptions in such efforts, as play movement leader Joseph Lee frequently pointed out, was that children are imitative by nature. They respond directly to the adult examples they see in their everyday life and model their behavior, to a surprising extent, after such examples. The recreation leader who worked with children, therefore, had to be, first and foremost, of sound moral character. The recreation leader was a model who led the difficult way, by example.

If ever there was a period in our history in which a return to such leadership was needed, this is it. As a previous section of this book documented, children are more likely to live in poverty than any age group, are as likely to reside with only one parent at some time prior to the age of eighteen as not, and appear to have been almost forgotten. Already, the plight of children and youth is becoming one of the most important political issues in our nation and a reform agenda is beginning to take shape. Leisure service professionals must be at the cutting edge of this issue. Society will empower such professionals to work with children and youth but, perhaps ironically, the credentials of the recreation, park and leisure service profession in regard to services for children may have to be re-established with the public. In recent decades, some recreation services to youth have been undertaken as merely diversion, keeping younger participants busy or off the streets. Other services to youth have been de-emphasized because those in positions of power thought they were expendable. All this is about to change and the leisure service professional must become more involved, and in different ways, in an old task that no one can do better. Leisure service professionals, as a group, exhibit personal character and styles of life which are likely to serve as the adult models Joseph Lee knew, many decades ago, that children needed.

What are the needs of children and youth that those in the leisure service profession must address? While they are too numerous to count, some of them are as follows. Children today need, first and foremost, to be taken seriously. That means treating them as children, not as adults or pets or as objects. They need to be paid attention to; we are ignoring them at our peril. Paying attention does not mean pushing them into the adult race for achievement and status, but it does mean listening, observing and planning.

Children need opportunities for play, which may mean "letting" them play rather than organizing their play, but letting them play in an environment which is safe and in which caring adults are present. Children also need opportunities to use skills they have learned in school rather than to be entertained. They do not need to be entertained — their most frequent use of leisure is the television. Children also need discipline. They need to be around adult leaders who are, as we used to say, "friendly but not familiar." To provide discipline, the child must not be the final arbiter of what happens. While it is important to try to understand the feelings and interests of the child, what children specifically don't need is a marketing approach to providing for them. They don't need to be asked what they want to do so much as they need to be shown models of what they can do or can learn to do. They also need to know what they must do to meet the expectations of adult leaders.

Leisure services will increasingly provide a means for youth to continue their learning or combine learning with other forms of recreation. Today's youth have a lot of catching up to do in terms of reading, math, science, geography, literature, history, and other areas of knowledge. Public leisure services can play a role in this endeavor, providing alternative learning environments from the school.

Children also need protection in our society. They are abused, left alone, ignored, and mistreated in a pathetic number of ways. Public leisure services must become, even more, advocates of children. They must be proactive on issues of child neglect, child care, and other issues. They must find ways to cooperate with Big Brother and Big Sister programs and other programs which benefit the welfare of youth. They must also find ways to deal with the issue of day care, whether or not they are the direct provider of such services.

As with every other change in leisure services, the issue of quality is critical in regard to youth services. No single service can afford to be a "babysitting" or "off the streets" program. To say a program seeks to get youth off the streets immediately raises the question of purpose. Children are different from adults. They do not have the same rights or privileges but they are as important. Recreation, park and leisure service professionals have a long proud history of working with youth. That history must now be remembered and acted upon.

Increasing Involvement in Tourism

Those in the leisure services will increasingly be involved in a number of aspects of tourism. This is coming about for a variety of reasons including the closer ties between public and private leisure services, the recognition that many leisure services organizations, such as state park systems, increasingly serve as a tourist destination, the recognition that recreation leaders in resorts fulfill many functions similar to those in the public sector, and the greater prevalence of tourists from other countries using public recreation and park facilities. Local park, recreation and leisure services will increasingly play a role in attracting tourists to their area as well as in local and regional attempts at economic development. Attracting industry and other employers will be increasingly dependent upon an area's perceived "quality of life," and public leisure services are, or should be, a critical variable in determining quality of life. Many of the quality of life issues, such as the existence of local festivals, exhibits, symposia and other special events, are not capital intensive but rather rely upon effective community organization. Many other quality of life issues will increasingly revolve around cleanliness, safety, other aspects of maintenance, architectural aesthetics, the existence of attractively planted flowers, trees, shrubs and other indicators of caring about community. Leisure services will be involved, or already are, in each of these undertakings. Certainly these issues are not new to leisure service professionals; they constituted part of the reform movement which industrialization brought about a few centuries ago.

International tourism is also growing, not only because of the advent of low-cost air transportation but also because of the increasing economic links between countries and an easing of political restrictions on international travel. Leisure service professionals will be involved here because much of such tourism involves ritual visits to scenic outdoor recreation areas and historic sites. Additionally, highly organized tours between countries will increasingly include plans for the "routine" recreation needs of the tourists, such as opportunities for exercise. Cultural exchanges between different nations will be more likely to involve specific communities and be locally organized, and such exchanges will involve the skills of those whom we currently call recreation programmers.

Tourism is already pushing leisure service professionals closer to those in the hospitality, hotel and restaurant industries. Many universities have already explored ways to academically link these areas more closely. Many hotel chains have developed "resort" hotels which are frankly leisure environments. Such environments serve not only as a primary tourist destination but also as an enjoyable place to stay for travelers who mix business and pleasure. To a remarkable extent, the success of such resorts depends upon the respect and attention the visitor is shown. Recreation and park professionals have a legacy of caring about people. Their transition to the commercial sector will be an easy one once they understand that one may contribute to the quality of an individual's life while working in a resort just as certainly as while working for a municipal leisure service agency.

Prevention — A Critical New Aspect of an Old Task

"Prevention" is an emerging key word in our society. As a concept, its importance has grown as we have come to realize that it makes economic, moral, and physiological sense to place our efforts more in preventing many situations we define as problems before they occur rather than attempting to remedy them after they have become visible. Part of this recognition is a more realistic view toward technology and science which, for a few decades, we had begun to believe could cure any emerging problems. Prevention also has become a crucial element in our thinking because our "mop up" approach to many problems has become so frightfully expensive that we cannot afford to pay for such "mopping up," even when it can be done. Prevention assumes that individuals must be taught to be increasingly responsible for their own actions so that they will come to freely choose behaviors which are good for them and for society. Such teaching involves presenting a rationale for the forming of certain ways of behaving. It often uses what Skinner (1978) called non-aversive conditioning. That is, the individual is rewarded for changing habits or behaviors which are deemed to be detrimental rather than punished for continuing them. One is encouraged to eat a low-fat diet which later will play a role in preventing the likelihood of heart attack. One is encouraged to read at a young age which will later be an important element in preventing the individual being unemployable. One is encouraged to learn to swim which may later prevent their drowning. One is taught a variety of leisure skills which may later prevent boredom or anti-social behavior.

While almost all the services provided by leisure services agencies have a preventative aspect, this aspect has not been seriously examined and communicated to the public. While a few "fitness" programs may do this, in many cases the prevention component goes unnoticed. Perhaps an example will demonstrate the many aspects of "prevention" which a leisure service can provide.

A few years ago I undertook a study with Dr. Michael Blazey of the use of urban neighborhood parks among citizens who were age 55 and older. More than 700 older park users were interviewed in 25 different local parks within five large cities. Some of the findings of this study demonstrate the case that can be made for the local park serving as a veritable "prevention center" for older users. The most frequent way older citizens got to such parks was walking. Additionally, they walked while in the park. More than one out of four were involved in some form of sport or other exercise while in the park. Over half participated in a non-sport activity such as bird watching. About one-half interacted socially with one or more other people while in the park. The park tended to be used as a part of routine for older users and about one-half of all users said they felt different about things after visiting the park. Overwhelmingly these changes were described as a positive emotional or mental change such as "a better outlook," "soothed," "like living when I get home," "healthier," "beautiful," and "now I can take a nap" (Godbey and Blazey, 1983). The park, as these data show, was a critical environment in dealing with a number of prevention issues. It enhanced behaviors which are positively linked to the prevention of a vast array of physical and emotional problems. If one calculated the health-related economic costs which society would incur had these parks not been available to older people, it might well be that local urban parks would be shown to be an extremely cost effective prevention strategy.

Such a line of reasoning will have to be taken with each and every service and facility provided by public leisure services. To a public which relies more on statistics than faith, documenting the extensive role of leisure services in preventing a number of health, social and environmental problems is critical.

The Need for Flexibility

While leisure services will have to operate within a value frame-
work more than they currently do, they will also have to be increasingly flexible. Flexibility is necessary since so many important components of even the short-range future are unpredictable.
These components are environmental, cultural, financial, spiritual
and others. While we can predict some societal changes such as
the age structure of the population or our near future financial debt,
there are many unknowns which will profoundly shape the next
decade. Environmentally, we cannot predict whether the depletion
of the ozone layer will lead to outlawing the use of petroleum in
internal combustion engines or make sunbathing as carcinogenic
an activity as smoking. A major earthquake in southern California
or a nuclear power plant disaster in India could alter economic
patterns for decades. The heating up of the earth could lead to the
disappearance of most of the earth's beaches and built environments on or near beaches.

Culturally, we cannot predict the impact of changing
women's roles, or those of men, as well as a changing ethnic mix
on leisure patterns. Nor can we tell how the human spirit will react
to our society's and the world's increasing interdependence.
Financially, while we are living dangerously above our means, a
sudden technological breakthrough or the increasing liberalization
in the Soviet Union and resultant cuts in military spending could
radically alter our economic future.

While the direction and magnitude of such change cannot
be predicted, change itself can be guaranteed. Our population,
economy, environment, our neighbors in the world, the growth rate
of knowledge are all changing at such a rapid rate that it is incon-
ceivable that the world will remain the same. In such a situation,
leisure services must be prepared to both respond to and initiate
change. This means organizational options must be kept open. No
employee should be led to believe his or her job will remain

unchanged for long, since no employee will have the luxury of sulking and refusing to cooperate when change occurs.

Flexibility will also mean increasing multipurpose design and use of existing leisure environments. As Dunn (1988) stated:

> In real estate, the three key concepts are location, location and location. In recreation planning, the triology of key ideas is flexibility, flexibility and flexibility. Let me elaborate. At my university, Penn State, we have a marvelous flexible facility called officially a golf course. It is a beautiful 36-hole course, nestled against both the university's main campus and its surrounding community. As you might expect, it provides opportunity for golf for the university students, faculty and staff, the citizens of the community, Penn State alumni, and tourists to the area. However, it is in fact a flexible facility. Throughout the year, one may see use being made of a track around and through the golf course by joggers, runners, walkers, people exercising dogs, and even bicyclists. Less active, but usually in evidence are the bird watchers and those with camera and tripod in hand. In the fall, the University's cross-country team trains there, and high school and college cross-country meets are held frequently. One may even see several of Joe Paterno's football players doing laps. Winter finds the golfers and their clubs in Florida or the Mediterranean, but the golf course is busy with cross-country skiers, snowshoers, and, when the white stuff is absent, those dedicated joggers and runners. Spring is one of my favorite times, for on the open space adjacent to the golf course is located an informal driving range, ball fields for intramural softball games, kite fliers, boomerang throwers (you thought that took place in Australia?) frisbee

tossers and even picnickers. Summer finds some of
these activities continuing, and as the season pro-
gresses, blackberry pickers, black walnut gatherers,
and the apple trees dispensing their harvest to those
who happen by. My point is simply this. Look for
the whole potential of sunk cost investments.
Think flexibility, flexibility, flexibility.

Such flexibility, of course, is an idea which is as ancient as
the British Commons but we will have to reinvent it, as Dunn
suggested, during the next few decades.

The Continuing Need for Entrepreneurship

Recreation, park and leisure services will continue to need entrepreneurship within the public sector because financially over-extended governments and a similarly overextended public, even though valuing leisure services, perceive them rather low on a hierarchy of needs compared to survival, food, shelter and health care. While the use of leisure is related to these concerns, there is ample evidence that Americans in the middle and upper classes can afford to and are willing to pay for specific recreation and leisure expenditures.

Entrepreneurship, however, means something much more fundamental than direct charges for services as opposed to the use of tax revenues. At its best, entrepreneurship means that a good idea results in a good product or service which benefits society at large, the developer of the product or service and the individual who had the idea. The public, or portions of the public, are willing to pay for the product or service because they recognize it as being worthwhile. All entrepreneurship, according to this way of think-ing, starts with ideas, not with imposing fees or merely looking for ways to make profit.

In the delivery of leisure services, increased entrepreneurial effort will have to start at the idea stage. These ideas will have to be based upon many types of information including constant contact with participants — and vision. Ideas are going to become the currency of future leisure services. Leisure always involves visions of the ideal, always addresses the question: Given a mini-mum of constraints, what is worth doing? Answers to this question are always acts of inspiration and those in leisure services will have to show inspiration. While leisure service professionals will become information users to an unprecedented extent, they will not succeed if such information does not lead to a vision, an opera-tional image of the ideal. The operational image of the ideal will be the basis for entrepreneurial effort. Suppose, for example, a leisure service professional begins to obtain information indicating that many older members of a community are interested in foreign travel. What visions come to mind? What scenarios can be developed to see if people are interested or can be interested? How about a year-long class devoted to the study of China, occasional meals with class members in Chinese restaurants, where class members get to know each other, followed by a trip to China that the class had jointly planned, step by step, with a local travel agent and members of the community who were of Chinese ancestry? What triggers such processes are visions of important, worthwhile leisure that have the potential to be made operational. It is ultimately the vision of future leisure service professionals that will determine our contribution and our professional fate.

The Increasing Need for Experimentation

Leisure services in both the public and private sector are entering a period in which experimentation in all facets of their operations is critical. New ways must be found of doing things and these new ways will, themselves, be subject to change. Experimentation can take place only in an environment which values ideas and which rewards those who carry out experiments even when they fail. Since many recreation, park and leisure service agencies are themselves becoming obsolete (failing), those who want to try out new visions within the agency can hardly be accused of bringing down the system.

Promoting experimentation must be understood as one part of a bigger issue — trusting employees. As management expert Tom Peters (1987) argued, if this change in attitude is to take place, the ideas of employees concerning ways to improve the organization must be given a hearing. If the process of developing urban parks as well as other recreation and park functions is one of "cultural discovery" rather than one of "technology" (Cranz, 1982), then the nature of leisure service organizations is inherently experimental, as are the services. Organizations which are experimental are particularly dependent upon the vision and actions of their employees, since the organization must be continuously reshaped and renewed to survive. Perhaps without stretching the point, it may be said that employees of leisure service agencies must have leisure. In keeping with the ancient Athenian notion of leisure, they must also be prepared to use such leisure through continuous education.

Employees, Peters (1987) maintained, must be viewed as the most important resource of an organization. Therefore, the process of hiring employees is critical and the educating and training of employees must be continuous and a top priority of the organization.

Part of the process of treating employees as the company's most valuable resource is to give them more authority and to trust them more. This may result in a decline in the number of employees in middle management positions, a removal of lots of red tape and less monitoring of employee behavior.

The Changing Role of Higher Education in Recreation and Leisure Studies

While universities have always been centrally involved in the preparation of students for leisure, through the various liberal arts, in this country concern for recreation and leisure has resulted in the creation of specialized curricula designed to prepare students for careers in various types of service, including outdoor recreation and education, therapeutic recreation, municipal recreation and park services, park planning and others. The growth of such curricula occurred during the 1960s and 1970s, when as many as 40,000 students majored in such subjects. The extremely rapid growth of such curricula was attributable to the entry of the affluent baby-boom generation into college and their interest in environmental issues, providing services to the urban poor and the handicapped, the appeal of public service and the prevalence of jobs within public sector recreation and park agencies. Universities promoted this rapid growth since such curricula were relatively easy to establish, low cost and, in many cases, provided a way for faculty from related curricula where enrollments were dropping, such as physical education, to continue their careers, often with no retraining. This growth resulted in the establishment and enlargement of a number of curricula which were intellectually suspect, understaffed, isolated from the rest of the university and oriented toward vocational preparation for entry level jobs within the public sector. While the National Recreation and Park Association began an accreditation project in an attempt to improve the quality of such programs, it was not until the approval of this accreditation program by the Council on Post-Secondary Accreditation in 1986 that the academic legitimacy of recreation, park and leisure studies within the university was determined. Paralleling such approval was both a decline in student enrollments in these curricula and an increase in the quality and academic rigor of a number of them. As employment in the public sector became scarce, enrollment declined in many such curricula, especially within associate degree programs which had been designed for training for direct entry into urban recreation leadership or other paraprofessional positions. Simultaneously, however, many curricula became increasingly integrated into the university. Several academic journals, including the Journal of Leisure Research, Leisure Sciences, Journal of Park and Recreation Administration, Therapeutic Recreation Journal, Recreation Research Review, Society and Leisure, Leisure Studies and others achieved legitimate status as refereed research journals. A number of professors within these curricula undertook programs of research, funded by a variety of sponsors. Courses were introduced or refined dealing with various aspects of leisure from the standpoint of sociology, psychology, geography, philosophy, history and other disciplines. Many non-majors began to enroll in such courses. A re-orientation took place within many curricula to preparation for employment in commercial recreation and tourism.

This process of change will be continued and intensified as universities respond to a changing society. The trend toward "basic" education within universities is likely to mean that recreation and park curricula, in their traditional form, will be de-emphasized or eliminated. Certainly they will be subject to close scrutiny during the next decade. A few such curricula which have recently undergone such scrutiny have emerged from the process higher in the esteem of university administrators, which is critical to their survival since the fate of such programs will be decided by those within the university, not recreation and park professionals. It is also likely that teaching coursework concerning the role of leisure in society and leisure services will be taught to more and more students who major in other subjects where the increasing importance of recreation and leisure is recognized. Such majors include hotel and restaurant management, forestry, marketing, physical education, special education, geography, natural resource management, and many others.

Professors within such curricula are also more likely to have diverse academic backgrounds, allowing for a frankly interdisciplinary approach to the subject to prevail. The teaching of majors for careers in the public sector may take a back seat to teaching those from other majors. In many institutions, the majority of majors in leisure studies may be, or already are, oriented to the commercial sector. Relations to business may be closer.

The need of recreation, park and leisure service professionals for continued education and for research will push educators into positions of power within professional organizations at a rapid rate. Young educators will increasingly be torn between public service and educational involvement with practitioners and more highly rewarded academic tasks such as publishing in research journals and obtaining external research funds.

It is in the area of continuing education that the biggest changes may take place. The survival of public recreation and parks as a profession is directly dependent upon the growth of opportunities for high quality opportunities for continuing education. Many universities either cannot or will not respond to this need for a variety of reasons, including archaic organizational structures, the belief that continuing education is of lesser academic status than research and publication, and lack of communication between university and professional organizations. This reluctance, if it continues, will likely lead to the establishment of new entrepreneurial organizations designed to fill this rather central gap. To its credit, the National Recreation and Park Association has made serious attempts to meet this need in the last few years.

Leisure Service as an Emerging Function of Diverse Organizations

As leisure has become a more central part of modern life, an increasingly diverse array of organizations will have a leisure component. There are already many examples. At the federal level, most land-managing agencies originally had no mission which involved leisure but gradually such a mission evolved. The U.S. Forest Service now recognizes "recreation" as one of the legitimate uses of government owned forest. The National Park Service has developed National Recreation Areas whose primary purpose is to provide outdoor recreation for those in surrounding urban areas.

Public schools have gone through a progression in which leisure, play and recreation first had no place in public education, a second phase in which they existed outside the formal curriculum (extracurricular activity) and a third phase in which they constitute a part of the curriculum.

In the near future, we will see a huge number of diverse organizations becoming more directly involved in leisure provision. Perhaps some examples will suffice. State highway commissions will more directly consider the leisure component of driving, visual aesthetics, the leisure behavior patterns of people who stop and rest during major trips, the kinds of information which can be effectively and safely transmitted to drivers about a host of local leisure amenities, from historical sites to tennis courts, which the driver is passing.

Public housing authorities will examine the suitability of design for children's play and the leisure needs of residents. There will also be training programs designed to acquaint and expose new residents of such housing areas to the leisure resources nearby and to prepare them to develop their own resources (such as public gardens) when such resources don't exist. Economic development councils and corporations, which try to entice industry to their communities, counties, or states, will increasingly be involved not only in identifying and promoting the leisure amenities of their areas to prospective companies which might relocate, but also in seeking to alter or expand the leisure amenities of their areas in accordance with the wishes of potentially relocating companies.

Hospitals will rethink every aspect of their environment from the standpoint of leisure expression. Certainly such experimentation has already begun. Hotels will increasingly function as leisure centers and the range of leisure services provided will center around not only hedonistic leisure pursuits such as dining, drinking, entertainment and sex but may include libraries, lectures, tours, sports, exhibits of arts and crafts and opportunities for peaceful contemplation while looking at panoramic views.

Many businesses, as part of the change in management philosophy from one of adversarial relations to one of cooperative relations, will become interested in recreation and leisure as a means of furthering such cooperation and strengthening individuals' identification with the company. Companies will also intensify their interest in promoting healthy forms of leisure expression among employees to minimize health insurance costs and lost time on the job.

Leisure services, in short, will be diffused through a greatly expanded range of organizations. As this happens, it will make increasingly less sense to think of a single government agency serving as a direct, comprehensive provider of "leisure services." Such a task would be too enormous to undertake, even to conceptualize. Public recreation, park and leisure services, then, will become increasingly both "enablers" and "facilitators." That is, they will assist, advise, coordinate, publicize, evaluate, support, "synergize," study, incubate, encourage, and otherwise indirectly shape the efforts of a vast array of private organizations.

While some version of the previous assessment has often been made, the implication of such changes are not yet adequately realized. The most important function of the public leisure service organization of the future will be the creation and dissemination of knowledge. Such agencies are currently ill-prepared for this role and will undergo rapid transformation and restaffing to achieve this change. The kinds of knowledge which such agencies will create and disseminate will include: (1) the conditions of the lives of residents, particularly the patterns and problems of their everyday lives, (2) the leisure patterns, values, and styles of residents and barriers to meeting leisure interests, (3) environmental conditions and the impact of the behaviors of residents on such conditions, (4) the existing and potential leisure resources of the area, both public and private, their qualities, interrelationships, current and potential users, logistics of use and future development, (5) the characteristics, motives and behaviors of tourists or other non-residents who visit the area and their leisure needs and interests, (6) the assessment of individuals and groups in the community concerning the qualities of their lives and their leisure, their visions for improvement, their complaints, sorrows, joys and fears, (7) the prevalence and nature of individual disabilities within the community which greatly restrict leisure expression and resources which minimize such restrictions.

Not only will all these types of knowledge need to be developed, they will have to be developed continuously rather than occasionally since the agency will serve, first and foremost, a "leisure monitoring function." This change in function will have enormous implications for higher education curricula in recreation, park and leisure services, in-service training of employees, and in measuring organizational success.

Promoting Environmental Improvement and Non-Consumptive Leisure Activity

During the next few decades, the leisure service profession must take a leadership role in discouraging forms of recreation and leisure which consume huge amounts of material goods and do harm to the environment. While from a marketing perspective one simply attempts to efficiently identify and supply what the public wants, the leisure service profession will have to seek to change behavior. That means, for instance, promoting sailing, canoeing and other forms of water recreation which do not consume petroleum rather than driving speedboats that have 500 horsepower engines. That means careful thought should be given as to whether national parks should develop extensive gift shops. That means walking and public transportation should be encouraged as ways to reach public recreation sites and the design of such sites should encourage this.

Perhaps for a second we should recall a bit of history. In the early days of the industrial revolution, those who owned the means of production saw the working class only as beasts of burden. What they did during their non-work time was of no concern.

> Only a handful of employers at this time understood that the worker might be useful to the capitalist as a consumer; that he needed to be imbued with a taste for higher things; that an economy based upon mass production required not only the capitalistic organization of production but the organization of consumption and leisure as well (Lasch, 1979).

Slowly, however, as the production system became capable of meeting basic material needs, the economy came to rely on the creation of consumer demands, "on convincing people to buy goods for which they are unaware of any need until the 'need' is forcibly brought to their attention by the mass media" (Lasch, 1979). Advertising, which previously merely called attention to a product or service and bragged about it, enlarged its purpose. "Now it manufactures a product of its own: the consumer, perpetually unsatisfied, restless, anxious, and bored. Advertising serves not so much to advertise products as to promote consumption as a way of life" (Lasch, 1979). Advertising has undertaken this task with such efficiency that we are now victims of our own wants, virtually never satisfied with what we own and at the same time poisoning the environment due to our ravaging of natural resources to perpetually try to satisfy such created wants.

Those in the recreation, park and leisure service profession have historically acted in opposition to this system of perpetually seeking to create new needs for commodities and experiences which could be purchased. Historically, the leisure activities which have been stressed have often required little in the way of facilities or equipment — summer playgrounds which used whatever public land could be found, athletic opportunities in which the equipment needs were minimal or were supplied and reused again and again, activities where everyone could participate regardless of whether or not they owned lots of expensive equipment.

The dilemma which leisure service professionals in the public sector now face is that they are increasingly asked to generate revenue through fees, charges and other means. Doing this appears to be most easily done by modeling after the commercial sector. The commercial leisure services, however, are often part of the process described previously which has led to a mindless consumerism. Shopping, in almost all commercial leisure enterprises, is the accompanying activity to a wide variety of leisure experiences that would appear to be satisfying and complete without shopping. Local festivals slowly emerge into selling festivals where "art" is bought rather than appreciated. Leisure experiences often seem not to exist unless there is an accompanying tee shirt documenting the event.

In the last decade, the commercial sector of leisure service has, in effect, led the public sector in terms of producing models to mimic. Part of this leadership reflects the traditional conservative leadership of public leisure services. Another part, however, would seem to be due to the diminished federal funding for public recreation and park systems and the resulting demand that such systems begin to "fund themselves" through a variety of methods. Public agencies, to support themselves, have begun such mimicking, often taking a marketing approach to services or turning over what they do to private companies.

While government at all levels is likely to change in the next decade to reflect the needs of a more dependent society, it is likely that public leisure services will continue to be asked to generate part of their operating costs, or, more accurately, the costs of government through revenue generation. This does not mean, however, that such services need to promote consumerism as previously discussed. It also does not mean that such services cannot operate with more of an environmental ethic, although there are obviously times when doing so will cost money, at least in the short term. While perhaps a bit cynical, it may be that many agencies will need to consider ways to generate revenue from having their areas and facilities serve as ecological models, rather than from making them copies of commercial resorts and shopping centers. The public's willingness to support high quality, environmentally sound services will have to be tested in the next decade and public park and recreation professionals must provide models for this testing. There must be the willingness to take chances, show daring, enunciate visions. There must be leadership which may have to limit park attendance, monitor or change the menu at snack bars, or interpret the environment to the public in ways that call for change. Interpretation will have to change drastically if it is to survive. Interpreting the natural environment will have to start where people live, demonstrate environmental consequences of our behaviors and suggest practical ways of changing behaviors at both a personal and a political level. If interpretation is merely a cute sideshow for park visitors, it deserves to be phased out. If interpretation does not make links between our world's increased population and the destruction of animal habitats, if it does not demonstrate the fundamental need to change our way of life, it can serve as no more than a cynical apology for a government dominated by special interests and multinational corporations. For environmental interpretation to regain its momentum, it will have to become instruction for change in the everyday life of those it reaches. To do less would be to ignore the body of knowledge that interpreters should possess.

EPILOGUE

This brief book is not so much about the future as it is about the present. It is based on the premise that our world is locked into a process of change and that such change must be accepted and managed as best we can. Not only has it been assumed that we must change, but also that we should. We have not recognized the nightmares of our era any more than a fish recognizes water. The problems and situations documented in this short book will mean immediate change in both our personal and professional lives. It will be immediately important not just to begin sorting the trash but to begin sorting out what kind of a response we will make individually and collectively, publicly and privately to the increasingly likely prospect that our way of life will change. What is required from you and each of us is vision. Ultimately that is what our profession has historically been about. Not what is but what can be, what should be. Not what is popular but what is right. Not "public relations" but a continuous relation with the public. Not services which divide but which join together. Not the slick defense of what exists but the translucent vision of what can be. Not the data from experts but the quiet understanding of the everyday life of those you serve.

Yet vision needs information to guide it. Vision divorced from information almost inevitably paves the road to Hell again with the same good intentions. For you and I and others in our field to create visions of what we can be, therefore, we need to relearn much about our society, economy and environment. We need to question. We need to grow.

Recently, ours has been a field that has quit taking risks. Given the trends outlined in this book, to continue to take no risks may ultimately be the biggest professional risk of all.

REFERENCES

Beck, V. 1987. Scientific Illiteracy Hurts U.S. State College, PA: *Centre Daily Times,* February 21.

Bengston, Vern L. and Dale Dannefer. 1987. Families, Work and Aging: Implications of Disordered Cohort Flow for the Twenty-First Century in Russell A. Ward and Sheldon S. Tobin (eds.) *Health in Aging: Sociological Issues and Policy Directions.* New York: Spring Publishing pp. 256-289.

Bennett, Georgette. 1988. *Crimewarps: The Future of Crime in America.* New York: Doubleday.

Best, Fred. 1980. *Flexible Life Scheduling: Breaking the Education-Work-Retirement Lockstep.* New York: Praeger.

Blake Weisenthal, Debra. 1988. When Nutritionists Speak, Not Many People Listen. *Vegetarian Times,* August, pp. 8-9.

Bloom, Allan. 1987. *The Closing of the American Mind.* New York: Simon and Schuster.

Brekke, Bo. 1988. Oil Reserves are Dwindling. *World Press Review*, January, p. 52.

Bryan, Hobson. 1979. *Conflict in the Great Outdoors.* University: Alabama, The University of Alabama.

Budd, Edward C. 1988. Quoted by David S. Martin, The Associated Press. Rich-Poor Gap Spreads Despite Working Women. State College, PA: *Centre Daily Times,* March 12.

Burdick, John. 1975. *Recreation in the Cities: Who Gains From Federal Aid?* Washington, DC: Center For Growth Alternatives.

Butsch, Richard. 1984. The Commodification of Leisure: The Case of the Model Airplane Hobby and Industry. *Qualitative Sociology,* 7(3), p. 217-229.

Capra, Fritjof. 1988. *Uncommon Wisdom: Conversations With Remarkable People.* New York: Simon and Shuster.

Carey, Max. 1981. Occupational Employment Growth through 1990. *Monthly Labor Review.* U.S. Department of Labor, Bureau of Labor Statistics, 104(8). Washington, DC: U.S. Government Printing Office.

Cherlin, Andrew J. and Frank Furstenberg. 1986. *The New American Grandparent.* New York: Basic Books.

Connell, Christopher. 1988. Quoted by The Associated Press. Extracurricular-Active Kids Make Grade. State College, PA: *Centre Daily Times,* June 27.

Cranz, Galen. 1982. *The Politics of Park Design: A History of Urban Parks In America.* Cambridge, MA: MIT Press.

Curtiss, Aaron. 1987. We All Pay Heavy Cost of Drug Use. State College, PA: *Centre Daily Times,* May 21.

Dannefer, Dale. 1983. Age Structure, Values and the Organization of Work: Some Implications for Research and Policy. *Futures,* 7:8-13.

Dentzer, Susan. 1988. "The Mega-Issues of the '90s," *U.S. News and World Report,* September 5, p. 59.

Diebold, John. 1987. Work Will Take A Back Seat to Leisure Time — 2010: Looking Into the Future World. Syndicated column quoted from *Centre Daily Times*, State College, PA, April 18.

Dunn, Diana R. 1988. *Leisure Trends and Forecasting: Planning the Future of Recreation.* Keynote Address. Alberta Association of the Canadian Institute of Planners and Alberta Association of Landscape Architects. Kananaskis Village, Alberta, Canada, May 20.

Edsall, Thomas Byrne. 1988. The Return of Inequality. *The Atlantic Monthly.* June, pp. 86-94.

Fitness Dropouts. 1988. *U.S. News and World Report,* July 18, pp. 14.

Furstenberg, Frank F. 1983. Some Implications of Divorce for Kinship Relations. Paper presented at the Eastern Sociological Society Annual Meeting, Baltimore, Maryland, March.

Garreau, Joel. 1981. *The Nine Nations of North America.* New York: Houghton-Mifflin.

Godbey, Geoffrey. 1985. *Leisure In Your Life: An Exploration,* 2nd Edition. State College, PA: Venture Publishing.

Godbey, Geoffrey and Michael Blazey. Old People In Urban Parks: An Exploratory Investigation. *Journal of Leisure Research ,* *15*(3), pp. 229-245.

Grof, Stanislav. 1976. *Realms of the Human Unconsciousness.* New York: Dutton.

Hardin, Garrett. 1968. The Tragedy of the Commons. *Science,* December 13, pp. 1243-1248.

Harris, Louis. 1987. *Inside America.* New York: Vintage Books.

Hewitt, Paul. 1986. Case Statement of Americans for Generational Equity. Washington, DC: Americans for Generational Equity.

Institute for Social Research, How Families Use Times. *ISR Newsletter*, Winter 1985-6, pp. 4-5.

Jackson, Jacqueline. 1971. Black Grandparents in the South. *Phylon 32*: 260-271.

Johnson, Warren. 1985. *The Future is Not What It Used to Be — Returning to Traditional Values In An Age of Scarcity.* New York: Dodd, Mead and Company.

Jones, Landon. 1980. *Great Expectations: America and the Baby Boom Generation.* New York: Ballantine.

Lamm, Richard D. 1985. *Megatraumas: America at the Year 2000.* New York: Houghton Mifflin.

LaPage, Wilbur. 1983. Recreation Resource Management for Visitor Satisfaction in Stanley R. Lieber and Daniel R. Fesenmaier (eds.) *Recreation Planning and Management.* State College, PA: Venture Publishing.

Lasch, Christopher. 1979. *The Culture of Narcissism — American Life In An Age of Diminishing Expectations.* New York: Warner Books.

Louis, Harris and Associates. Cited by Marilyn Adams. *USA Today*, December 4, 1984, p. 1A.

Masnick, George and Mary Jo Bane. 1980. *The Nation's Families: 1960-1990*. Cambridge: Joint Center for Urban Studies of MIT and Harvard University.

McHale, John. 1978. The Emergence of Futures Research in *Handbook of Futures Research*, edited by Jib Fowles. London: Greenwood Press.

McLuhan, Marshall. 1964. *Understanding Media: the Extensions of Man*. New York: Signet Books.

Moynihan, Daniel Patrick. 1976. Social Policy: From the Utilitarian Ethic to the Therapeutic Ethic in Commission on Critical Choices, *Qualities of Life*, Lexington, MA: D.C. Health.

Naisbett, John. 1982. *Megatrends —Ten New Directions Transforming Our Lives*. New York: Warner Books.

Owen, John D. 1969. *The Price of Leisure*. Rotterdam: Rotterdam University Press.

Peele, Stanton. 1978. Addiction: The Analgesic Experience. *Human Nature*, September, pp. 61-67.

Peters, Tom. *Thriving on Chaos: A Handbook for a Revolution in Management*. New York: Random House.

Pollock, Linda. *A Lasting Relationship: Parents and Children Over Three Centuries*. London: Fourth Estate, 1987.

Rifkin, Jeremy. 1987. *Time Wars: The Primary Conflict in Human History*. New York: Henry Holt and Company.

Sagan, Carl. 1977. *The Dragons of Eden — Speculation on the Evolution of Human Intelligence*. New York: Random House.

Sagan, Carl. 1988. The Common Enemy. *Parade*, February 7, pp. 4-7.

Skinner, B. F. 1978. *Reflections on Behavioralism and Society*. Englewood Cliffs: Prentice-Hall.

Sussman, Marvin B. 1985. The Family Life of Older People in *Handbook of Aging and the Social Sciences*, R. Binstock and E. Shanas (eds.) New York: Van Nostrand Reinhold. pp. 415-449.

Toffler, Alvin. 1980. *The Third Wave*. New York: William Morrow and Company.

United States Census Bureau, reported by Randolph E. Schmid, The Associated Press, April 5, 1988.

United States Department of Labor. 1988. *Work Force 2000*. Washington, DC, March.

Wolfenstein, Martha. 1955. Fun Morality in *Childhood in Contemporary Cultures*. Edited by Margaret Mead and Martha Wolfenstein. Chicago: University of Chicago Press.

Yankelovich, Skelly and White, Inc. 1982. The Impact of Changing Values on Leisure. (Unpublished) November.

OTHER BOOKS FROM
VENTURE PUBLISHING, INC.

The Future of Leisure Services: Thriving on Change, by Geoffrey Godbey

Planning Parks for People, by John Hultsman, Richard L. Cottrell and
     Wendy Zales-Hultsman

Recreation Economic Decisions: Comparing Benefits and Costs, by
     Richard G. Walsh

Leadership Administration of Outdoor Pursuits, by Phyllis Ford and
     James Blanchard

Leisure in Your Life: An Exploration, Revised Edition, by Geoffrey Godbey

*Acquiring Parks and Recreation Facilities through Mandatory Dedication:
     A Comprehensive Guide,* by Ronald A. Kaiser and James D. Mertes

Recreation and Leisure: Issues in an Era of Change, Revised Edition, edited
     by Thomas L. Goodale and Peter A. Witt

Private and Commercial Recreation, edited by Arlin Epperson

Sport and Recreation: An Economic Analysis, by Chris Gratton and
     Peter Taylor (Distributed for E. and F. N. Spon, Ltd.)

Park Ranger Handbook, by J. W. Shiner

*Playing, Living, Learning—A Worldwide Perspective on Children's
     Opportunities to Play,* by Cor Westland and Jane Knight

Evaluation of Therapeutic Recreation through Quality Assurance, edited by
     Bob Riley

Recreation and Leisure: An Introductory Handbook, edited by Alan Graefe
     and Stan Parker

The *Leisure Diagnostic Battery—Users Manual and Sample Forms,* by
     Peter A. Witt and Gary D. Ellis

Behavior Modification in Therapeutic Recreation: An Introductory Learning Manual, by John Dattilo and William D. Murphy

Outdoor Recreation Management: Theory and Application, Revised and Enlarged, by Alan Jubenville, Ben W. Twight and Robert H. Becker

International Directory of Academic Institutions in Leisure, Recreation and Related Fields (Distributed for WLRA)

Being at Leisure—Playing at Life: A Guide to Health and Joyful Living, by Bruno Hans Geba

Amenity Resource Valuation, edited by George L. Peterson, B.L. Driver and Robin Gregory

The Evolution of Leisure, by Thomas L. Goodale and Geoffrey C. Godbey

Leisure Education: A Manual of Activities and Resources, by Norma J. Stumbo and Steven R. Thompson

Risk Management in Therapeutic Recreation: A Component of Quality Assurance, by Judith Voelkl

Beyond the Bake Sale: A Fund Raising Handbook for Public Agencies, (Distributed for City of Sacramento, Department of Recreation and Parks)

Gifts to Share: A Gifts Catalogue How-To Manual for Public Agencies, (Distributed for City of Sacramento, Department of Recreation and Parks)

Venture Publishing, Inc.
1640 Oxford Circle
State College, PA 16803
(814) 234-4561